summer flush
July to September

beans (French;
  runner)
broccoli (Calabrese)
bunched beetroot
bunched onions
cabbage (Hispi)
celery
chard
chillies
courgette
cucumber
fennel
globe artichokes
  and cardoons

lettuce (Batavia;
  cos; Little Gem)
pak choi
peppers
potatoes (Marfona;
  Cosmos)
salad leaves
samphire
spinach
sugar snap peas
sweetcorn
tomatillos
tomatoes
watercress

spring
and
summer
veg

RIVERFORD
ORGANIC FARMERS

guy watson

with kirsty hale, anna colquhoun, rob andrew
and other riverford cooks

To the customers whose trust allows us
to farm and do things the right way

16

32

44

58

72

88

88

98

112

126

138

154

174

192

208

222

240

242

244

246

250

254

256

contents

And if you can't find any of
the veg below in this book, it's
because you'll find them in our
Autumn and Winter Veg book:

Beetroot, Celeriac and Salsify
Brussels sprouts
Cabbages and Kale
Carrots, Parsnips and Swede
Cauliflower and Romanesco
Jerusalem artichokes
Leeks, onions and garlic
Potatoes
Purple sprouting broccoli
Radicchio/other bitter leaves
Squash and pumpkin

introduction

the book

I want this book to bridge the gap between aspiration and reality; to make a turnip or courgette exciting and to prevent a cardoon or artichoke from being intimidating. My dream is that a veg box will seem like an allotment without the work, and that this book will help make veg the stars of your eating. Most of the recipes are quick and simple, with lots of variations, suitable for those weekday nights when you're tired but want to get something on the table that's good, seasonal and in budget. Our cooks have not been able to resist a few more challenging ones, which I hope will appeal to the more seasoned and less time-pressed cooks among you. Our intention is above all to make veg box cooking easy and pleasurable. I hope that in a year's time, your copy of this book will be grubby, dog-eared and stained beyond recognition.

farm and kitchen

My four siblings and I grew up watching and helping my father farm and my mother cook and garden. Growing, preparing and sharing food was the arranging force of our lives.

My mother was a fantastic cook who drew her inspiration from the ingredients in the hedgerows or produced on our mixed Devon farm and in her garden. She was deeply unfashionable: in the 1950s and '60s, as the nation emerged from the tedium of post-war food rationing to embrace the exotic (which came in tins, cans, jars and bottles), her cooking celebrated seasonality, provenance and tradition. We wanted Hellman's but she made mayonnaise from her own eggs, baked infuriating bread that crumbled under often rancid homemade butter, and made her own bacon and preserves. On top of raising five children and countless calves and chickens, this was a feat that would have been fêted by today's foodies (and feminists), though I suspect she would not have appreciated their attention.

My father wasn't from farming stock. He was restlessly experimental and, like many pioneers, frequently incompetent. The parish and his neighbours didn't expect him and his innovations to last, but he demonstrated dogged determination and proved them wrong. The farm was run from the kitchen table, giving us all a keen appreciation of the tribulations of business. We learned as much from his failures as from his triumphs, and watched as he lost faith in the post-war rush to intensive farming and sought a better way. Above all we absorbed his optimistic belief that anything was possible with enough drive.

Six decades after he came to Riverford, after a little experimentation in the outside world, all five of his offspring are back on the farm: Ben who runs the farm shop and a very creative production kitchen, two dairy farmers (Oliver and Louise), my sister Rachel (whose idea this book was) and me, still as obsessed as I was as a child with growing and selling vegetables.

veg boxes

I started growing vegetables in 1986 with an ancient borrowed tractor, a wheelbarrow and a field next to our farmhouse. After 30 years of trial and error, Riverford now packs and delivers veg boxes across the country. It's been a rollercoaster ride of insane gambles and hard work, but it feels like a blink since I was picking ingredients from the garden with my mother, washing the mud from them at the sink and waiting hungrily for her to transform them into a feast-like supper for the family and farm staff. Essentially nothing has changed; the veg box scheme is all about sharing the seasonal best, when the veg is as fresh as possible, with the minimum of fuss, packaging and marketing.

spring to summer – gathering abundance; slowly

Each season brings its excitement and pleasures in the kitchen; spring starts with scarcity, then abundance and variety rise gradually to a late-September crescendo. The first salads and greens are sown under cover early in the new year; in a good year we might risk planting some potatoes in a few favoured fields in February but planting does not really get under way until late March, leaving an annual 'hungry gap' when our customers' appetite for root veg and stews is waning but the new crops haven't yet yielded. To make matters worse, cookery writers and celebrity chefs, wanting to be the first to feature a vegetable, are generally a month or even two ahead of the real season.

Perennials, with the help of an established root system, give us the first vegetables of the season; we start picking asparagus, rhubarb, wild garlic and my beloved cardoons in April. Even with our mild climate in Devon and the help of fleece covers to advance crops we don't start picking lettuce, salad greens, first early potatoes and strawberries until mid May. By June a new crop is starting every week – even after 30 years I still find myself getting excited by the first broad beans. Real abundance hits in mid July when we pick the first tomatoes, and the season reaches its peak in September, when we often struggle to find a home for all this plenty in the boxes.

I reckon a truly committed and experienced seasonal cook could eat 90 per cent UK-grown vegetables without hardship, but 20 years of looking into customers' and friends' fridges in March has taught me that most people don't manage it. We've settled on a pragmatic compromise to maintain variety in the boxes while the new season plantings mature, importing from our farm in France and direct from growers we know and trust further south, mainly in Spain. Research we have done with Exeter University suggests it can be 20 times less environmentally damaging to import a Spanish pepper than to buy one from heated glass in the UK. But we never airfreight and enjoy the UK season to the full.

riverford cooks

Notwithstanding all the cooking on TV, the glossies and recipe books, cooking is hard if you didn't grow up around it – and many people didn't. Back in the 1990s, when I delivered the first boxes to friends and family, it quickly became obvious that some customers needed a helping hand. With my mother's aid I created sporadic recipe newsletters, photocopied at the last minute. Just as my repertoire was getting exhausted, we opened the Field Kitchen, our farm restaurant, and I was able to call on a real chef for help.

Riverford Cooks is a determined, if absurdly utopian, plan to address the reality gap between celebrity chefs proclaiming their enthusiasm for seasonal veg in the media and people really learning how to enjoy practical, affordable cookery at home. It's a loose affiliation of professionals and proficient amateurs who share our style of cooking and enthusiasm for seasonal veg and give informal classes to our customers. The major contributions to this book have come from Kirsty Hale, creator of the recipes that come with our veg and recipe boxes; Anna Colquhoun, a founder Riverford Cook; and Rob Andrew, ex-head chef at the Field Kitchen. Thanks to them all, and a good few others besides, who have contributed time, knowledge and recipes to this book.

Guy Watson

the riverford cooks

The eclectic mix of cooks and chefs who work with Riverford have one thing in common: an enthusiasm for cooking with fresh seasonal produce and making vegetables the star of the plate. Riverford's founder **Guy Watson** is an enthusiastic amateur cook who has honed his skills over 25 years cooking veg for breakfast, lunch and dinner. He is supported by the chefs in our farm restaurant (the Field Kitchen) and and London organic pub (the Duke of Cambridge) and a community of professionals inspired by the quality of the farm's produce and style of cooking, who devise the recipes for the boxes and work up and down the country at Riverford events. Below is an introduction to a few of those who have contributed to this book. Thank you to all the others who have sent us ideas and recipes over the years. Please keep them coming.

Kirsty Hale is something of a recipe legend at Riverford. Resolutely dubbing herself a cook rather than a chef, Kirsty has been devising the weekly and seasonal collections of recipes that give inspiration to our veg box customers for many years, as well as running cooking events and food demonstrations and conjuring up menu ideas for Riverford's new recipe boxes. Kirsty is a champion of simply cooked, seasonal food that never compromises on flavour, with a bias towards vegetarian cooking (although she's not one!).

Anna Colquhoun, aka The Culinary Anthropologist, is a cooking teacher, food consultant and writer with a fascination for the anthropology of food. Something of a food nerd, Anna has travelled far and wide to research her subject, having first trained as a chef in San Francisco and at Alice Waters' legendary restaurant, Chez Panisse, in Berkeley. She continues her anthropological studies and research at the School of Oriental and African Studies in London. Anna is author of Eat Slow Britain; consultant on BBC Radio 4's The Kitchen Cabinet and is Riverford's preserving guru. She offers cooking classes in London, including popular bread-making and preserving workshops. Her supper club, the Secret Kitchen, is a convivial dinner at which people share a surprise seasonal menu. Anna is also renovating a stone farmhouse in Croatia where she will host culinary holidays. *www.culinaryanthropologist.org*

Rob Andrew is becoming a Riverford fixture. He joined us to head up the enormously popular Travelling Field Kitchen (housed in a yurt), and then took over as head chef at the stationary version on the farm in Devon – the pioneering Riverford Field Kitchen. Rob's grounded but creative culinary background suits our philosophy of good food and good farming. His experiences include working in a seafood restaurant in Melbourne, living off-grid on an organic smallholding in Tasmania and working as part of the vibrant restaurant scene in Brighton.

Guy
Watson

Kirsty
Hale

Anna
Colquhoun

Rob
Andrew

store cupboard essentials

Different cooks need different store cupboards. The list below will help transform your veg box and will put you well on the way to making the most of the recipes in this book.

grains, seeds and pulses

* Dried pasta and noodles

* Rice (long grain, basmati, Arborio)

* Couscous and/or bulghur wheat

* Lentils (Puy and a red or yellow split lentil)

* Flour (plain and self-raising; gluten-free absorbs more liquid so recipes may need a splash more if you use this)

* Quinoa

tins and jars

* Tinned chickpeas, white beans (cannellini, haricot or butter) and red kidney beans

* Tinned tomatoes (we generally find chopped the most useful)

* Tomato purée/concentrate

* Mustard (English/Dijon and/ or wholegrain)

* Olives (in brine or oil)

* Capers (in brine or salted)

* Anchovies (in oil or salted)

* Tinned coconut milk

bottles

* Oils (good-quality extra virgin olive oil for salads and drizzling; light olive oil for roasting or frying; sunflower or rapeseed oil for frying at high temperatures)

* Vinegars (red wine, white wine and balsamic)

* Soy sauce (use tamari for gluten-free)

* Worcestershire sauce (Biona do make an organic vegetarian version)

flavourings

* Ground spices (use as fresh as possible for the best flavour and grind whole spices, if you can get them, in a pestle and mortar or spice/coffee grinder; an ✿ indicates where we think whole are best): caraway seeds✿, cardamom pods✿, coriander✿, chilli flakes, cinnamon (whole sticks and ground), cumin seeds✿, medium curry powder, fennel seeds✿, mustard seeds✿, nutmeg✿, paprika (unsmoked and smoked sweet), saffron threads

* Dried herbs (bay leaves, mint, oregano [or marjoram], thyme)

* Fine and coarse or flaky sea salt

* Peppercorns

* Sugar (caster, soft light brown and dark muscovado)

* Honey

* A good vegetable bouillon for making a quick stock, if you're short of time)

fridge

* Parmesan (or vegetarian alternative; and/or other hard cheeses)

* Feta, halloumi and a soft sheep's or goat's cheese

* Lemons and limes

frozen

* Stock (chicken, beef and/or vegetable; stock cubes will do but fresh/frozen stock is usually better)

* Pastry (puff and shortcrust)

Kitchen kit

You can tackle most vegetables with a sharp knife and a sturdy chopping board. Below are a few other recommended items for your vegetable tool box.

* Good vegetable scrubber

* Big, heavy, sharp cook's knife for chunky veg like squash

* Small serrated knife for tomatoes

* Swivel peeler (for potatoes)

* Box grater (for cheese and veg)

* Very fine, sharp grater or Microplane (for Parmesan, horseradish, ginger, citrus zest and nutmeg

* Stick blender (for blitzing soups)

* Kitchen paper (for draining vegetables and fried food)

* Salad spinner (to get salad leaves dry without mess)

* Pestle and mortar (for grinding spices and smashing garlic)

* Potato ricer or masher

* Cast-iron griddle pan (for griddling; especially useful if you do not have a good oven grill)

* Mandolin (for thinly slicing veg; very useful for gratins amongst other things)

june to november

artichokes
and
cardoons

Since founding the farm, I have indulged a 25-year obsession with these prickly relatives of the thistle without ever managing to turn a profit. I live in hope but have to acknowledge that the preparation required, the often bitter earthiness and occasional toughness mean that they will not be for everyone. Artichokes, and in particular, cardoons, vary hugely in bitterness, sweetness and toughness according to variety, maturity at picking and growing conditions. They are both native to north Africa and are grown around the Mediterranean in large quantities where they are eaten as a staple winter vegetable.

In the UK globe artichokes (not to be confused with root or Jerusalem artichokes, which feature in the Autumn and Winter volume of this series) are in season in June and July from an established crop, or September to November from a spring planting. Boiling these is a good start though their flavour is at its best when fried.

Cardoons, much beloved by Victorian gardeners, are cultivated for their fleshy leaf ribs and are most tender in spring but can be in season at almost any time. If you have a large garden to fill and are a lazy or poor gardener, cardoons are for you. Once established, their vigorous habit and impressive stature (up to 3m) mean they are able to shade out any weed.

Guy

artichokes and cardoons

storage

Artichokes are best eaten straight after picking, but they'll keep well in a plastic bag in the fridge for up to four days. A good specimen has a tight leaf formation and feels heavy for its size.

Store cardoons in a plastic bag in the fridge and use within a week. If they're too long for your fridge, cut them in half and discard the shrivelled part.

prep

Large artichokes suit boiling, steaming or stuffing. Small artichokes are usually more tender and good for trimming down and braising. Clean artichokes by sitting them upside down in a big bowl of water for a minimum of 10 minutes, allowing any dirt to sink. If you're in a rush, a quick rinse under a tap will do. The cut surfaces of artichokes discolour quickly, so put them into a bowl of cold water acidulated with a good squeeze of lemon juice or a splash of white wine vinegar.

Cardoon stalks require a bit of effort and you will need to watch out for their prickles. Wear disposable gloves if you have them, which will also protect your hands from staining brown. Cardoons also discolour once peeled, so put them into a bowl of acidulated water as above. First separate the stems if they are still joined and remove the big leaves. Discard any damaged outer stalks. Some people also discard the stalks in the very centre too, since they are particularly bitter. Then run a sharp knife down both edges of the stalks, removing the line of small leaves and spines.

Next use a small knife or peeler to pare away the tough, fibrous outer layer and strings which run lengthways all around the convex side of the stalk. Finally, cut the stalks crossways into 2–6 cm crescents and put them straight into the acidulated water.

eating artichokes raw

You can eat a very fresh artichoke raw just as you would a boiled one – leaf by leaf, scraping the flesh off the bottoms with your teeth, then removing the choke and eating the base. Alternatively, trim the artichoke down to its heart and slice it finely to toss into a salad. Make the vinaigrette first so that the prepared slices can go straight into it before they have time to discolour.

cooking

We usually boil artichokes and then eat them leaf by leaf, dipped into melted butter, mayonnaise or vinaigrette. This is slow but satisfying, and culminates in the reward of the tender heart. When there is more time and baby artichokes are in season, we trim them down and braise them with lemon juice and olive oil. The braised hearts are particularly tasty and have a multitude of uses (see page 20). For special occasions, we stuff large artichokes or deep-fry baby ones.

braise the hearts

If you have a lot of artichokes, this takes a bit of effort at the preparatory stage, but it's worth it.

* Pull away the outer leaves, breaking them off as near to the base as possible. Keep going until the lower half of the remaining leaves are cream coloured and tender rather than green and hard.

* Lay the artichoke on its side and cut off the top with a sharp knife, leaving just the cream-coloured bottom section.

* Trim the stalk and base, cutting away the tough green outer layer and leaf stubs to reveal the paler flesh beneath.

* Cut the artichoke into quarters lengthways. Use a teaspoon to scrape out the hairy choke. Keep the prepared hearts in a bowl of acidulated cold water until they're all ready to cook (see page 18).

* Place in a large saucepan and cover the quartered artichokes with roughly equal parts of water, white wine, lemon juice and olive oil, seasoned with salt. There should be just enough liquid to keep them submerged. For a lighter flavour, use plain water with the juice of a lemon, or for added complexity, throw in a couple of bay leaves, a sprig of thyme, peppercorns, sliced garlic and a dried chilli for a little kick.

boil or steam

Cut off the artichoke stalk. Bring a large saucepan of salted water to the boil and add the juice of a lemon or a few tablespoons of white wine vinegar. For a different flavour, throw in a bay leaf and a couple of peeled garlic cloves. Lower the artichokes upright into the pan and simmer for 30–45 minutes. When they're ready, a leaf should come off easily and the fleshy base will feel tender when bitten.

To steam, put a few centimetres of water in the pan and cook for the same time with the lid on. Check the water doesn't boil away.

Let the cooked artichokes drain upside down in a colander for a few minutes then serve while still warm, or eat them cold dressed with a little vinaigrette.

* Simmer gently until the artichokes are tender, 20–40 minutes depending on their size. Lift them out and then boil their braising liquid until it thickens slightly, though watch it doesn't become salty as it reduces. Store the artichokes in their liquid; they will keep for up to five days in the fridge, or longer if you bottle them in sterilised jars.

WAYS TO USE BRAISED ARTICHOKE HEARTS

* With peppery leaves, Parmesan shavings, boiled eggs, cooked prawns, new potatoes and anchovies. Toss with a lemony dressing (see page 261).

* Blitz in a food processor, adding enough braising liquid to make a coarse paste. Use as a dip or spread on toast. Add grated Parmesan, cream cheese and/or mayonnaise, spring onions or chives, and maybe some extra lemon juice and crushed garlic. A dash of Worcestershire or Tabasco sauce will add oomph.

* Arrange in a gratin dish and pour over a ladle or so of reduced braising liquid. Cover with a mixture of breadcrumbs, crushed garlic, grated Parmesan and parsley. Drizzle over a little olive oil and bake at 180°C/Gas 4 for around 25 minutes, until bubbling and golden.

* Slice and toss with pasta; fold into a risotto, along with butter and Parmesan; or add to a frittata or quiche.

stuff

Trim the base so the globe sits upright, then lay the artichoke on its side and use a sharp knife to cut off the top third. Pull out the inside leaves, leaving an outer layer of leaves to contain the stuffing. Use a teaspoon to scrape out the hairy choke so the heart beneath is exposed. Rub with lemon juice or vinegar to prevent discolouration. Fill the cavity with stuffing. Try some of the following ideas, or for more detailed recipes, turn to page 24:

* Fried onions, bacon and mushrooms mixed with breadcrumbs and herbs (see page 23 for which ones work well with artichokes)

* Ricotta mixed with Parmesan, hard-boiled egg and herbs

* Chopped olives, anchovies, garlic, breadcrumbs and herbs

Once stuffed, braise the artichokes by putting them snugly in a heavy-bottomed saucepan with a good glug of olive oil. Add liquid (water or stock, perhaps with some white wine and herbs) to a depth of 2–3cm. Cover with a lid and simmer over a low heat or in a low oven (160°C/Gas 3) until the artichokes are cooked, around 1 hour or so, depending on size. The cooking liquid could then be boiled to reduce and served as a sauce.

An alternative approach to stuffed artichokes is to boil the artichoke whole as described opposite and then remove the inner leaves and choke. Serve the artichoke filled with mayonnaise or a cold salad; crab and prawn salads work well.

cooking cardoons

Cardoons are bitter and tough when raw and so need to be boiled or braised before being used in a dish. To simply boil them, add the prepared cardoon pieces (see page 16) to a big saucepan of well-salted boiling water and boil until completely tender, which will take anything from 15 minutes to 1 hour depending on their size and age (the time can really vary this much!). Pull one out every so often and test it with a knife. When tender, drain and cool. Cooked cardoons can be stored in the fridge for up to 5 days.

artichokes and cardoons work well with...

* acid – lemon juice, white wine, vinegar
* anchovies
* cured pork – bacon, chorizo, prosciutto
* dairy – butter, cheese, cream
* eggs
* garlic
* green summer veg – broad beans, green   beans, peas
* herbs – bay, chervil, chives, mint, parsley, tarragon, thyme
* mushrooms and truffles
* shellfish – especially crab and prawns

IDEAS FOR USING COOKED CARDOONS

* Place the cardoons, along with cooked potatoes, celery and/or globe artichoke hearts in a buttered gratin dish, pour over a little cream, stock or white sauce (béchamel), top with a grated hard cheese or breadcrumbs and bake at 180°C/Gas 4 for around 45 minutes until bubbling and golden.

* Cardoons are particularly good in a Moroccan-style chicken tagine along with olives, preserved lemon, turmeric, ground ginger and fresh coriander, or try them stirred through a beef, lamb or vegetable stew.

* Fry onions and garlic as usual then add the cardoons and stock, with maybe a potato or two to give body. Blend and serve with a drizzle of truffle oil if you are lucky enough to have some.

* Dress the cardoons with a vinaigrette (see page 260) and serve at room temperature.

stuffed artichokes

We don't tend to overload our customers with artichokes as they seem to be a minority taste and send out the odd couple, now and again. But they are often available to add to your order if you particularly like them. One of the easiest ways to prepare artichokes is to boil them whole before cooling then stuffing them, or to stuff then bake them. Here are a few of our favourite ideas.

cold stuffed with crab, chilli and lemon

quick & easy

SERVES 4

4 large artichokes, boiled whole, trimmed
   and cleaned for stuffing (see page 21)
200g mixed white and brown crab meat
½ red chilli, deseeded and finely chopped
small blob of mayonnaise or aioli
small bunch of parsley (or a mixture
   of tarragon and parsley), chopped
½ lemon
salt and black pepper
buttered bread and salad leaves, to serve (optional)

In a bowl, mix together the crab meat, chilli, mayonnaise and parsley. Season to taste with lemon juice, salt and pepper.

Spoon into the artichokes. Serve with buttered bread and salad leaves.

cold stuffed with eggs, capers and green herbs

quick & easy

SERVES 4

4 large artichokes, boiled whole,
   trimmed and cleaned for stuffing (see page 21)
2 tinned anchovy fillets, finely chopped
½ garlic clove, finely minced
½ tbsp red wine vinegar
1 tsp Dijon mustard
2 hard-boiled eggs, peeled
½ tbsp capers, roughly chopped
1 tbsp chopped parsley
¼ tbsp chopped tarragon
30g Parmesan, grated
olive oil
salt and black pepper
warm cooked Puy-style lentils to serve (optional)

Mix the anchovies, garlic, vinegar and mustard together in a bowl.

Roughly chop or grate the hard-boiled eggs. Add to the bowl together with the capers, herbs and Parmesan and give it a good mix. Add enough olive oil to loosen to a spoonable consistency. Check the seasoning and adjust if necessary.

Spoon the mixture into the artichokes. Serve with warm Puy-style lentils if wished.

baked with Parmesan, ham and breadcrumbs

long slow cook

SERVES 4

4 large artichokes, prepared for stuffing
    and baking (see page 21)
100g fresh sourdough breadcrumbs
100g sliced ham, prosciutto or salami
50g Parmesan, grated
1 garlic clove, finely chopped
2 tsp oregano
olive oil
salt and black pepper

Heat the oven to 160°C/Gas 3.

Put the breadcrumbs, ham, Parmesan, garlic
and oregano in a food processor and pulse
until finely chopped. Add a drizzle of olive
oil until the mixture is loosened and moist.

Check the seasoning then stuff into the
prepared artichokes and bake as described
on page 21, uncovering for the last
20 minutes to brown the tops.

baked with ricotta, walnuts and spinach

long slow cook

vegetarian (if you use
vegetarian cheese)

SERVES 4

4 large artichokes, prepared for stuffing
    and baking (see page 21)
1½ tbsp walnuts
1 garlic clove, finely chopped
100g spinach, blanched, squeezed
    and roughly chopped (see page 180)
300g ricotta
¼ grated nutmeg
½ lemon
salt and black pepper

Heat the oven to 160°C/Gas 3.

Pulse the walnuts and garlic in a blender
or chop into a coarse paste on a board.

Fold the walnuts and the spinach into the
ricotta. Add the nutmeg and season with
salt, pepper and a squeeze of lemon juice.

Stuff into the prepared artichokes and
bake as directed on page 21, uncovering
for the last 20 minutes to brown the tops.

artichokes with spring veg and new potatoes

quick & easy

vegetarian
(if you use veg stock)

Somewhere between a soup and a stew, this goes well with some good rustic bread grilled and rubbed with garlic and olive oil. If your sunny afternoon clouds over, we'd recommend adding the dash of cream.

SERVES 2

dash of olive oil
1 onion, diced
1 celery stick, diced
2 large artichokes cut
  and trimmed for braising
  (see page 18), each cut
  into 8
6 new potatoes, scrubbed
  and cut into 1 cm dice
2 garlic cloves, finely chopped
generous knob of butter
1 glass of dry white wine
1 bay leaf
1 thyme sprig
400ml hot chicken
  or veg stock
handful of blanched, podded
  and skinned broad beans
handful of peas
50g washed baby leaf spinach,
  roughly chopped
dash of cream (optional)
small handful of parsley,
  chopped
1 lemon
salt and black pepper

Heat a little oil in a saucepan and gently fry the onion and celery over a low heat for 5–10 minutes until starting to soften.

Add the artichoke and potato, season with a pinch of salt and sauté for a few minutes, keeping the veg moving.

Add the garlic and butter and fry for a couple of minutes until the garlic smells fragrant and the butter is foaming and turning slightly nut brown.

Pour in the wine and add the bay leaf and thyme sprig. Let it bubble until reduced by half.

Add the chicken stock and bring to a very gentle simmer. Cover loosely with a lid and leave to simmer for about 20 minutes – the artichokes should be tender and the potatoes still holding their shape but easily crushed against the side of the pan with a spoon.

Add the broad beans, peas and spinach. Stir through gently and let the spinach wilt for a few minutes. Now would be the time to add the cream if you're using it.

Season well. Add the parsley and finish with a squeeze of lemon juice, it will take more than you'd think.

chicken, artichoke and olive tagine

long slow cook

freezable

A lightly spiced tagine which you can easily scale up for a large gathering. Good with a bowl of fluffy couscous.

SERVES 2

2 large chicken legs, thighs
   and drumsticks separated
olive oil
1 large onion, sliced
2 garlic cloves,
   finely chopped
1 preserved lemon
bunch of coriander
1 tsp ground coriander
1 tsp ground cumin
1 tsp ground ginger
pinch of saffron threads
30g pitted green
   olives, halved
2 artichokes
300ml hot chicken stock
salt and black pepper

Heat the oven to 160°C/Gas 3. Season the chicken pieces with salt and pepper. Heat a little olive oil in a casserole, add the chicken pieces and fry on a medium heat until nice and golden brown on all sides.

Add the onion and garlic and continue to fry gently for 5 minutes.

Remove the seeds and pulp from the preserved lemon and discard. Slice the peel into thin strips. Chop the coriander stalks roughly, reserving the leaves for later, and add to the casserole with the sliced lemon peel, coriander, cumin, ginger, saffron and olives. Fry gently for 2 minutes to release the fragrance from the spices.

Pour over the stock and bring up to a simmer. Give it all a good stir to release any sticky bits from the bottom of the casserole. Cover with a tight-fitting lid or some foil and place in the oven for 40 minutes.

Meanwhile, trim and prepare the artichokes ready for braising (see page 20) and cut each into 8.

Remove the chicken from the oven, taste the liquid and add more salt and a few grindings of pepper if you think it needs it. Add the artichokes, stir gently, put the lid back on and return to the oven for a further 40 minutes.

Remove from the oven. The meat should just be slipping from the bone and the artichokes tender to the tip of a knife. Taste and adjust the seasoning. Serve scattered with the reserved coriander leaves.

cardoons with lentils

quick & easy

Simple and satisfying, this dish uses just a few ingredients to make a hearty vegetarian meal. Or serve it as a side dish for roasted meat - it's particularly good with lamb.

SERVES 4

olive oil
400g onions, thinly sliced
600g cardoons (see page 18)
   cut crossways into
   1–1.5cm crescents
glass of dry sherry (optional)
250g Puy or green lentils,
   rinsed in a sieve under
   cold water
4 garlic cloves, skin on,
   halved crossways

Place the lentils and garlic in a saucepan. Cover with plenty of cold water, bring to the boil and simmer for about 25–30 minutes, or until soft.

Meanwhile, fry the onions in 2 tablespoons of oil over a low–medium heat, stirring now and them, until they're just starting to colour – about 15 minutes.

Add the cardoons to the onions and cook for another 20 minutes or so, until soft. Season and add the sherry, if using.

Drain the lentils, reserving some of the cooking water. Squeeze the garlic cloves out of their skins over the lentils. Add the lentils and garlic to the onions and cardoons. If the mixture looks dry add some of the reserved cooking water. Season with salt and pepper to taste and serve.

Guy's cardoon gratin

easy

vegetarian
(if you use vegetable
stock)

In his desire to convert the world to cardoons Guy has tried out various recipes on friends and family. This one passed muster with them all. Serve as a starter, main or side, depending on how many mouths you're feeding. Add some potatoes to feed a few more.

SERVES 4-6

250ml double cream
500ml chicken or veg stock
1 bay leaf
1.5–2kg cardoons
    (about 1 large or
    a few smaller ones)
100g Gruyère or similar
    hard cheese (Cheddar
    will do), grated
salt and pepper

Put the cream, stock and bay leaf in a large saucepan and season with salt and pepper.

Prepare the cardoon as described on page 18 – you needn't be too fussy for this recipe. Cut it into 1–1.5 cm crescents, crossways to the fibres, placing them immediately into the cream mixture as you go to stop them discolouring.

Bring the pan to a simmer and cook, stirring occasionally, until the cardoons are tender, which can take up to 1 hour.

Transfer to a gratin dish, discard the bay leaf, sprinkle with the cheese and bake at 180°C/Gas 4 for about 30 minutes, or until golden and bubbly.

aspara-gus

may to june

For an organic farmer, asparagus is the ultimate challenge; weeds being the problem. Asparagus' tall wispy foliage never casts enough shade to suppress weeds, while its unruly growth habit makes row cultivation difficult. For the cook however, it is a delight and an iconic marker of the start of another season; all I ask is that you savour each mouthful.

The UK season starts in late April and runs to late June, when the crop must be left to replenish its roots if it is to crop the next year. Should you find yourself at a vegetable market in the Mediterranean in the winter, look out for bunches of spindly, foraged wild asparagus; a much stronger tasting version of the cultivated crop, it is one of the best things I have ever eaten.

Guy

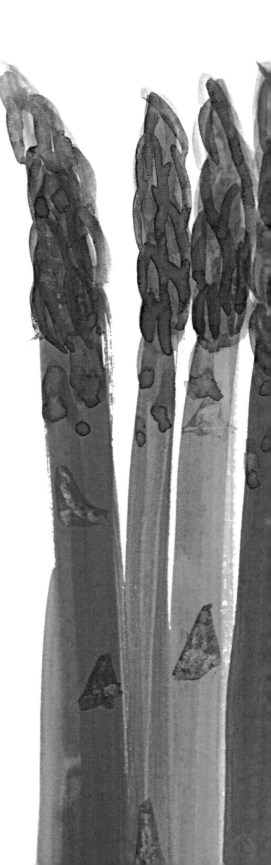

asparagus

storage

Enjoy your asparagus as soon as possible – preferably within a day or two. After asparagus has been picked, the shoot keeps growing, using up its sugars and getting less sweet and juicy. Keep it fresh in a glass of water in the fridge until you are ready to eat it.

> ### REVIVING AGEING ASPARAGUS
>
> Trim a centimetre off the bottom of the stems and stand them in a glass of water with a couple of teaspoons of sugar stirred in. Leave in the fridge for a few hours to help the stems firm up and regain a bit of sweetness.

prep

Asparagus stems develop woody bases, so snap these off first. Bend each stalk and it will break at the point where the toughness ends. Don't waste the bases – they are good for flavouring stock: bash each piece with the flat side of a large knife to crush it and release its flavour, then add to the stockpot. If you follow chefs who peel the bottom part of the stem to ensure perfect tenderness (we usually don't), then the peelings can go in too.

eating asparagus raw

Really fresh asparagus can hardly be improved by cooking. For a fresh-tasting and simple salad, prepare some firm, fat stems as above, shave thinly with a good veg peeler and dress with salt, lemon juice and olive oil. Good additions include freshly podded peas, Parmesan or goat's cheese, rocket or spinach leaves, and a few toasted pine nuts or hazelnuts. Boiled eggs turn this into a complete meal.

cooking

Asparagus cooks in a matter of minutes. Blanched or grilled and combined with just a few other ingredients, it makes a speedy and delectable supper. Its short cooking time also means it can be added to stews, risottos and pasta sauces just before they're done.

blanch

This is the easiest cooking method, and possibly the best way to preserve asparagus's distinct taste. Boil the stalks in a wide pot of well-salted water for 2–4 minutes, testing frequently, until tender to the tip of a knife. Fish the spears out with a slotted spoon or tongs (dropping them into a colander may harm the delicate tips) and drain well.

Blanched asparagus needs nothing more than a pat of good butter, some sea salt and perhaps a squeeze of lemon, or a hollandaise sauce if it's a special occasion. If you're not eating it immediately, plunge it into cold water to stop the cooking and preserve the bright colour. Once cold, the asparagus can be kept in the fridge and served later in a salad, or reheated with a knob of butter.

griddle

Griddling works best if the asparagus is blanched for just a couple of minutes first (see above), though it should still be crisp. Refresh in cold water and spread on a clean tea towel to dry. Heat a cast-iron griddle pan over a high heat until very hot. Rub the asparagus with oil and salt and lay on the griddle pan at a right angle to the ridges. Cook for 2–3 minutes on each side until tender and branded with griddle marks.

Serve warm with poached or fried eggs or cool as part of a salad – try it with griddled courgette and halloumi with a lemon and basil dressing.

roast or grill

This is a good way to cook large batches of asparagus, and since it takes longer to cook than on the stove, you run less risk of accidentally under- or over-cooking it. Heat the oven to 210°C/Gas 7. Rub the asparagus all over with oil and salt and lay in a single layer on a baking sheet or in a roasting tin. Roast on the top shelf of the oven until the asparagus is tender and starting to caramelise, about 8–12 minutes, depending on thickness.

This method also works under the grill, and will take just minutes, depending on the ferocity of your grill; turn the asparagus halfway through.

Roasting or grilling provides an opportunity to add flavourings: lemon zest and grated Parmesan both work well – add them about 5 minutes before the asparagus is done. Rashers of bacon or halved tomatoes, roasted or grilled, also go well.

fry

You can fry sliced asparagus in butter or oil over a medium heat until tender – only a few minutes – and then add them to beaten eggs to make an omelette or frittata. Or stir-fry finely sliced asparagus in a wok over high heat with other finely sliced tender vegetables such as mangetout and peppers. Try finishing the stir-fry with soy sauce, sesame oil, lime juice and crushed toasted peanuts.

works well with...

* butter
* eggs
* lemon
* mint
* mushrooms, also black truffles
* new potatoes
* nuts – hazelnuts are particularly good
* orange
* Parmesan
* peas
* pine nuts
* prosciutto and bacon

asparagus, broad bean and herb risotto

quick & easy

vegetarian (if you use an
alternative to Parmesan)

This is a basic risotto packed with spring veg and fresh herbs.
Cooking the rice in the oil for a couple of minutes before adding
any liquid opens up the grains so they release their starch and
absorb more stock, which gives the dish a creamier texture.
Adding butter and cheese at the end adds richness. Everyone
has a favourite texture to their risotto, so make yours firmer
or slightly sloppier, depending on your preference.

SERVES 4

2 tbsp sunflower or light
  olive oil, for frying
100g butter
1 large onion, finely diced
2 large garlic cloves,
  finely chopped
350g risotto rice
1 large glass (250ml)
  dry white wine (or just
  use a little more stock)
2.5 litres hot veg stock
700g broad beans in
  their pods
2 bunches (400–500g)
  of asparagus, snapped to
  remove the woody stems,
  stalks chopped into small
  pieces (leave the spear
  ends slightly longer,
  about 4–5cm)
100g grated Parmesan or
  vegetarian alternative
2 handfuls of chopped
  herbs (e.g. parsley, mint,
  chervil, tarragon)
salt and black pepper

Heat the oil and half the butter in a large, heavy-bottomed pan.
Add the onion and fry for 10 minutes, stirring, without colouring.

Add the garlic and rice and cook, stirring constantly, for 2 minutes,
until the grains turn translucent. Pour in the wine, if using, and
simmer until the liquid has been absorbed, then add the hot stock
a ladleful at a time (you may not need all of it), stirring the rice
often. The rice will take 20–25 minutes to become al dente
(tender but still with some bite).

Meanwhile, pod the broad beans. In a pan of boiling water, cook
the beans for 4 minutes. Drain, plunge into a bowl of cold water
to refresh, then drain again. Peel off the outer skins (see page 60–1).
Set aside.

When the rice is almost cooked (after about 20 minutes), add
the asparagus. Cook for a further 3–4 minutes, depending on its
thickness. The rice should be cooked, but still have some bite. Add
the broad beans, the rest of the butter and half the cheese. Season
to taste. Stir, turn off the heat, cover and leave to sit for 2 minutes.
Stir in the herbs and sprinkle over the rest of the cheese.

VARIATIONS
The basic recipe can be adapted with lots of veg: try adding
blanched greens or beans, fried or griddled courgette, roasted
aubergine and pepper, braised fennel, shredded wet or wild garlic,
or both. You could also add fried lardons or leftover roast chicken.

roasted asparagus with spring onions and goat's cheese

quick & easy

vegetarian (if you use
vegetarian cheese)

We serve this dish as a starter in the Field Kitchen. It is simplicity itself and makes a perfect lunch with a few slices of chewy, crusty bread and butter. We use a goat's cheddar as it lends itself well to grating, crumbling or shaving, but a younger, fresher goat's cheese will still hit the mark.

SERVES 2

1 bunch of asparagus
olive oil
4–6 spring onions,
   depending on size
50g goat's cheddar
½ lemon
salt and black pepper

Heat the oven to 210°C/Gas 7. Snap the tough lower stalks from the asparagus then split any larger stems in half lengthways so that they are all roughly the same size.

Toss the asparagus in a baking dish in just enough oil to coat. Season with salt and pepper and roast in the oven for 8–12 minutes (depending on thickness) until just tender.

Trim the spring onions; nip off the root, cut off the darker ends and peel away the first layer of skin. Slice very finely at an angle. Break up the slices with your fingertips.

As soon as you take the asparagus out of the oven, squeeze the lemon juice over it and toss the spring onions through.

Pile on to a plate and crumble, grate or shave the cheese on top.

VARIATIONS
* New season bunched onions can be used instead of the thinner spring onions; thinly slice the bulbous base of the onion and divide up the rings.
* Use a soft, fresh crumbly sheep's cheese, such as Sussex Slipcote, or a Feta-style cheese or some shavings of pecorino.

new potato and chorizo hash
with asparagus and egg

quick & easy

SERVES 2

600g new potatoes,
    scrubbed and cut in half,
    or in quarters if larger
sunflower or vegetable oil,
    for frying and roasting
250g asparagus, trimmed
splash of sherry vinegar
    or red wine vinegar
½ tsp smoked paprika
1 red onion, finely diced
2 cooking chorizo sausages
    (200–250g), skinned
    and meat crumbled
handful of finely
    chopped parsley
splash of white wine
    vinegar or cider vinegar,
    if poaching your eggs
2 eggs
salt and black pepper

You can either fry or poach your eggs for this recipe. Use the freshest eggs for making poached eggs, so the white seals around the yolks (adding the vinegar helps with this too).

Heat the oven to 210°C/Gas 7 or heat a cast-iron griddle pan over a high heat.

Put the potatoes in a pan of salted water, bring to a boil and cook for 12–15 minutes, until tender. Drain and lightly crush with a potato masher or fork.

While the potatoes are cooking, if you want to poach your eggs, put another pan of water on to heat to a bare simmer (no bubbles).

Toss the asparagus in 1 tablespoon of oil in a baking dish. Add a splash of sherry or red wine vinegar, the smoked paprika and season with salt and pepper. Roast in the oven for 8–12 minutes (depending on the thickness), until tender.

Heat 1 tablespoon of oil in a frying pan. Add the onion and cook slowly for 10 minutes to soften without colouring. If it starts to catch, add a splash of water and reduce the heat. Add the chorizo, increase the heat slightly and fry for 4–5 minutes, to cook the chorizo through. Stir in the potatoes and warm through. Stir in the parsley and season to taste.

If poaching your eggs, add a good splash of vinegar to the simmering pan of water. Crack the eggs into individual ramekins or small bowls. Use a spoon to swirl the water so it looks like a whirlpool. Gently drop the eggs into the water, one at a time, and poach for 3 minutes. Alternatively, fry the eggs in a little oil to your liking.

Sprinkle the eggs with a little extra salt before serving on the potatoes and asparagus.

green minestrone with mint and pesto

quick & easy

vegetarian (if you use
a vegetarian alternative
to Parmesan)

This soup celebrates the vibrant green veg around in early summer. If you're missing some of them, just use more of the others instead. Riverford Cook Anna uses this recipe when teaching knife skills as all the veg need to be cut into even dice. The mint and the pesto topping really lift the soup, so don't leave them out; but you can use shop-bought pesto to save time.

SERVES 6

250g thin asparagus
approx. 1.5 litres good
   vegetable stock
Parmesan rind
approx. 3 tbsp olive oil
4 celery sticks
2 medium onions
2 garlic cloves, crushed
4 potatoes
1 medium courgette
200g fine green beans
200g peas, podded
   (fresh or frozen)
1 small head of spring/
   summer greens, ribs cut
   out, leaves finely shredded
30g mint, leaves picked
150ml double cream
salt and black pepper

For the pesto (or use shop-bought)
75g pine nuts
1 small garlic clove, crushed
200g basil leaves
75g Parmesan or vegetarian
   alternative, finely grated
approx. 250ml extra virgin
   olive oil
lemon juice, to taste
salt and black pepper

Snap off the tough stem ends of the asparagus and bash them with the flat of your knife to crush them. Add to the stock along with the Parmesan rind; these will add flavour. Heat the stock to a gentle simmer. Cut all the veg except the greens into 5mm dice.

In a large saucepan, heat the olive oil and add the celery and onion and a pinch of salt. Fry slowly over moderate heat until soft but not coloured, about 10 minutes, stirring frequently. Add the garlic halfway through. If the pan seems dry, add a dash more oil or a splash of water. Add the potatoes.

In a bowl, mix all the prepared green vegetables with your hands. Add half of this mixture to the pan, along with another pinch of salt, and stir. Add enough stock to the pot to just cover the vegetables, bring to the boil, then simmer for around 20 minutes, or until the potatoes are tender.

Make the pesto. Lightly toast the pine nuts in a dry frying pan. Put the pine nuts, garlic, basil and Parmesan in a food processor and blitz. Drizzle in the olive oil and blitz again until it forms a loose paste (you may need more or less oil depending on the consistency you like). Season with salt, pepper and lemon juice, to taste.

Add the greens to the soup, along with more stock or water if needed so that they stay submerged. Simmer for 5 minutes then remove from the heat. Cut the mint leaves into fine ribbons: stack several leaves, roll up the pile and then cut it crossways into thin strips. Stir the mint and cream into the soup and season to taste. Serve warm with a dollop of pesto on top. Any leftover pesto will keep for several days in the fridge. Place in a jar and cover the top with a layer of olive oil.

july to october

auber-
gines

The Italian classic, aubergine parmigiana (baked aubergine with cheese, or Parmesan aubergine, if you're being literal with the translation) is one of my all-time favourite dishes (find the recipe on page 53), and aubergines are a really versatile veg – a sponge for all kinds of flavours. I just wish that they grew better in our climate. We have tried, but without artificial heat (which we consider environmental madness), even under plastic or glass their season is vanishingly short. Almost our entire crop comes from Spain, for which I make no apology as they have a lower carbon footprint and taste better than 99 per cent of those grown in the UK.

Guy

aubergines

storage

Unblemished, aubergines should last well in the salad drawer for up to four days. Use them while they're still smooth-skinned and firm and feel heavy for their size; once they've turned wrinkled and flabby, they may taste bitter.

prep

Wash aubergines just before preparing them then cut off their stem and leafy cap.

to peel or not to peel?

The skin is edible but, although it looks nice, can be unpleasantly tough even once cooked. If you're deep-frying, it's best to remove it all. If you're shallow-frying or grilling it, there is no need to peel. Keep the skin on for stuffed or charred aubergines (see pages 56 and 48). A useful halfway house is to 'pyjama' the aubergine: use a vegetable peeler to remove lengthways strips of skin, leaving your aubergine striped. This works well for roasted and fried aubergine chunks.

to salt or not to salt?

Many old recipes tell you to salt aubergines to draw out the bitterness. Modern aubergines have been bred to be less bitter, so this is generally no longer necessary. However, if you intend to shallow- or deep-fry it, salting is still a good idea: this draws out the water so that the aubergine won't absorb as much oil as it fries.

To salt, toss the chunks or slices with a good sprinkling of fine salt and leave them to sit in a colander for an hour. Give them a quick rinse or wipe them with kitchen paper to remove the salt before cooking.

cooking

Aubergine can be fried, grilled, roasted, baked or boiled. Pretty much the only thing you can't do with it is eat it raw, so whatever cooking method you choose, make sure it's not undercooked – it should be meltingly soft right to the centre.

fry

TO PAN-FRY Cut the aubergine into smallish slices or dice and cook them in a moderately hot pan with a dash of oil, stirring frequently until cooked through and starting to colour, about 6–10 minutes depending on the size of the pieces. Add more oil if needed: they soak it up. Stir in some garlic, chilli and tomato towards the end of the cooking time and eat with pasta and parmesan or pecorino for a quick supper.

TO DEEP-FRY Peel, cube and salt the aubergine (see above) and make sure the chunks are dry. Heat oil to 180°C in a deep fat fryer and cook the aubergine in batches until tender and nicely coloured. Lift the aubergine out with a slotted spoon on to a wad of kitchen paper to absorb the excess oil. Each batch will take only a few minutes.

TO SHALLOW-FRY Prepare the aubergine as for deep-fried but then cook it in a single layer in about one centimetre of heated oil in a wide frying pan. Fry over medium heat until the aubergine is a rich golden colour underneath, then carefully flip over the pieces and continue frying until they are cooked through. You could dust with spices (paprika, cayenne and cumin are good) before cooking and serve with lemon wedges to squeeze over.

grill/griddle

You can use a barbecue, a heated cast-iron griddle pan or a baking tray under a heated overhead grill. Slice the aubergines quite thinly, rub all over with olive oil and salt and cook for a few minutes on each side over a moderate heat (nothing too fierce or they'll blacken before they cook through). They should end up juicy, soft and nicely branded with charred lines (unless cooking under your grill).

Sprinkle with garlic, oil, lemon zest and herbs (mint, parsley and basil all work well); or drizzle with tahini, pomegranate molasses and runny honey. Grilled aubergine pairs beautifully with lamb.

roast

'Pyjama' your aubergines (see page 4–6), cut into bite-sized cubes, batons or half-moons and toss with a generous drizzle of olive oil and some salt. Spread over a roasting tin or baking tray and cook in an oven heated to 200°C/Gas 6 until completely tender and starting to caramelise – about 30 minutes.

Avoid overcrowding the tin or they'll steam rather than roast. Give a gentle toss halfway through cooking.

Alternatively, cut the aubergines in half lengthways, score the insides with a criss-cross pattern, tuck sliced garlic into the slits if you like, drizzle generously with oil and sprinkle with salt. Roast flesh side up in an oven heated to 200°C/Gas 6 for about 40 minutes or so, until soft to the core and nicely coloured. Enjoy as they are, or top with sliced tomatoes and mozzarella and return to the oven for another few minutes until the cheese has melted.

IDEAS FOR ROASTED AUBERGINES

* Mix with couscous and other roast vegetables for a hearty salad. Drizzle this with yoghurt and harissa (a moroccan chilli sauce) for a spicy kick.

* Toss with pasta, fried garlic, grated Parmesan and torn basil leaves for supper. You could roast some cherry tomatoes for this at the same time as the aubergines.

* For an Asian-style side dish, toss with lightly fried garlic and spring onion, soy sauce, rice wine vinegar, sesame oil and toasted sesame seeds.

* For a Georgian-style salad, let the aubergines cool, then roughly chop and mix with coarsely ground walnuts, finely diced red onion, chilli flakes, parsley, coriander and vinegar.

aubergines

bake

Aubergines feature in much-loved baked dishes around the world, including Italy's melanzane alla parmigiana, Greece's moussaka and Turkey's imam bayaldi (literally, 'the priest fainted' – so good is it). In most cases, the aubergine needs to be pre-cooked (usually fried) before being assembled for baking. (See our recipe for baked aubergine with spiced lamb on page 56.)

simmer/steam

As a fresher alternative to frying or roasting, try simmering or steaming large chunks of peeled aubergine for 10 minutes or so until tender. Allow the aubergine to drain well, or the dish will be watery. Dress with vinaigrette, or with minced garlic, white wine vinegar, olive oil, parsley and black olives. Serve at room temperature as a side dish.

For a Japanese flavour, cut slits into the skin sides of large unpeeled chunks of aubergine, simmer in a broth pepped up with flavourings such as dashi, soy sauce, sake, mirin and ginger, allow to cool in the broth and then serve at room temperature.

char

This is a popular way to prepare aubergines – the blackened skin gives the soft flesh a gorgeous smoky flavour. There are several methods, but leave on the stem and leafy cap for all of them. The first gives the smokiest flavour:

* Place the whole aubergine directly onto a gas burner. The flames should lick the aubergine as it rests on the pan supports. Use tongs to turn it over occasionally so that the whole skin blackens. It should take 10–15 minutes, and should feel like a bag of air when prodded, yielding no resistance. Don't rupture it with your tongs or its juicy insides will make a mess.

* Heat the oven grill to high. Cut several small slits in the sides of the aubergines so they don't explode, place them on a foiled baking sheet and cook under the grill until charred on the outside and deflated, turning them several times during cooking to ensure they blacken evenly. This will take around 30 minutes or more; their insides need to be totally soft.

* Heat the oven as hot as it will go (220–250°C/Gas 7–9). Cut little slits in the aubergines so they don't explode, then bake until blackened and collapsed. This may take up to an hour. Turn halfway through cooking. To speed things up you could halve the aubergines lengthways and cook them flesh side down on an oiled baking sheet.

In all cases, let the charred aubergine cool in a bowl for a few minutes, then peel away the blackened skin and remove the stem. Very occasionally, the juice released when cooling is unpleasantly bitter – taste to check. If so, break the flesh up a little in a colander and let any remaining juice drain away.

Once mashed up your smoky pulp is ready to use:

* For a baba ghanoush dip for flatbreads, mix the pulp of 2 aubergines with 2 tablespoons of tahini, 2 tablespoons of olive oil, the juice of 1 lemon, 2–3 crushed garlic cloves, a small handful of chopped mint or parsley or both, a dash of pomegranate molasses if you have any, or fresh pomegranate seeds, a pinch or 2 of dried chilli flakes (optional), then season and add more lemon juice or olive oil to taste.

* Use the pulp to make soup with slow-fried onions, plenty of garlic and some stock. Eat with a swirl of cream.

KEEPING THE COLOUR

Cut raw aubergine is prone to discolouring. If you're not going to use it immediately, toss the pieces with a little lemon juice. The pale soft pulp from charred aubergines (see above) is also prone to darkening. To keep it creamy, sprinkle with lemon juice as soon as you have peeled away the blackened skin.

works well with...

* Asian flavourings – chilli, ginger, mirin, miso, soy sauce
* Cheese – especially feta, halloumi, mozzarella, Parmesan
* Garlic
* Lamb
* Pomegranate and pomegranate molasses
* Sesame – oil, seeds, tahini
* Summer herbs – basil, coriander, mint, parsley
* Sweet and sour flavourings – lemon juice, vinegar, honey, sugar
* Tomato
* Walnut

grilled aubergine, feta, olive and mint salad

quick & easy

vegetarian (if you use
vegetarian feta)

A summer favourite of Riverford Cook Anna. Serve this salad at room temperature to enjoy the flavours at their best. Grilling the aubergines on a barbecue would be even better, heightening their smoky flavour.

SERVES 8

about 6 tbsp pine nuts
2 garlic cloves, crushed
  to a paste
5 tbsp balsamic vinegar
150–200ml extra virgin
  olive oil
3 aubergines, sliced
  lengthways 5mm thick
approx. 160g feta, crumbled
good handful of black olives,
  e.g. Kalamata, pitted
  and halved
handful of basil leaves
handful of mint leaves
salt and black pepper

Lightly toast the pine nuts in a dry frying pan, tossing them frequently, until golden. Make a dressing by whisking the crushed garlic with the vinegar, olive oil and salt and pepper to taste. How much oil you need will depend on the strength of your balsamic vinegar, and personal taste. Go easy on the salt as the feta and olives will all be a little salty anyway.

Heat a cast-iron griddle pan until very hot. Brush or rub the aubergines with some of the dressing (just enough to coat on both sides) and grill them in batches until they are soft to their centres and have nice grill marks, about 3–4 minutes on each side.

Assemble the salad by layering the aubergine with the pine nuts, feta and olives and drizzling the remaining dressing over as you go. Finish by tearing or finely slicing the basil and mint leaves and scattering them over the top.

VARIATION
You could also make this recipe with grilled courgette strips.

aubergine pasta sauce

quick & easy

vegetarian (if you use
a vegetarian alternative
to Parmesan)

freezable

SERVES 2

flesh from 1 large or
   2 small charred aubergines
   (see page 48)
2 tsp olive oil
additions of choice
   (see method)

The soft flesh you're left with after charring and peeling
the aubergine makes the perfect base for a silky smooth
pasta sauce. Use shaped pasta rather than spaghetti for
this – it has more nooks and crannies to hold the sauce.

Set your pasta to cook in a large saucepan of boiling salted water.
In a separate pan, beat the olive oil into the aubergine flesh over
a low heat, turning it until glossy and loose. Let your creativity
(or the contents of your store cupboard!) guide you with additions
such as:

* A dash of cream and some finely crushed garlic: warm through
and fold into the pasta. Finish with a squeeze of lemon, shredded
fresh basil or parsley and grated Parmesan.

* Some capers and chopped olives, a couple of chopped anchovy
fillets and a small ladle of passata or tomato sauce: stir into the
pasta and finish with some fresh oregano, mozzarella and
chopped red chilli.

aubergine parmigiana

quick & easy

vegetarian (if you use
vegetarian cheese)

freezable

SERVES 2

600g passata (sieved
   tomatoes) or tomato
   sauce (see page 226)
2 aubergines, sliced 5mm–
   1cm-thick, and shallow-
   fried (see page 47)
2 small bunches of basil
small bunch of oregano
125g Parmesan or vegetarian
   alternative, grated
200g mozzarella

This Italian classic of baked aubergines layered with tomato and
cheese is Mediterranean comfort food at its best. It is a meal in
its own right, though also makes a sumptuous side dish for simple
grilled meats or a roast. Some mozzarella contains animal rennet,
so if you are vegetarian, source one without.

Heat the oven to 180°C/Gas 4.

Spread a layer of passata or tomato sauce in a shallow ovenproof
dish. Cover with a layer of prepared aubergines, some torn basil
leaves, a few oregano leaves and a sprinkling of Parmesan. Add
alternate layers of passata, aubergine and herbs until all have been
used up. Top with a generous layer of torn mozzarella and a final
handful of Parmesan and bake for 20–30 minutes, until the top
is blistered and erupting.

miso-glazed aubergines

quick & easy

vegan

SERVES 2

2 tbsp miso (brown or white)

4 tbsp mirin

2 aubergines, split and
  roasted in halves
  (see page 48)

1 tbsp sesame seeds,
  lightly toasted

Miso is a salty fermented paste made from soy beans and wheat or rice, with a unique and slightly addictive flavour, although as with Marmite; you love or hate its saltiness. Miso can be used as a marinade, or added to liquid to make a broth. It is readily available in large supermarkets and Asian grocers and there are different types – white miso being the sweetest. The paste often comes in packets or pots, ; it keeps for a while but if you find it coming to the end of its fridge shelf life before you've used it all, freeze in ice cubes trays or small tubs.

Serve this with sticky rice, a simple salad or coleslaw with an Asian dressing, or with wilted pak choi or summer greens.

Mix the miso, mirin and 1 tablespoon of water in a small bowl or mug. Put the roasted aubergine halves flesh side up on a baking sheet and smear with the miso mixture. Grill under a medium grill until the miso is golden. Scatter with the toasted sesame seeds.

baked aubergine with spiced lamb, mint and pomegranate

a bit fancy

1 large aubergine
sunflower oil or light olive
    oil, for frying and roasting
25g flaked almonds
1 onion, finely diced
1 large garlic clove, finely
    chopped or crushed
300g minced lamb
2 tsp ground cumin
1 tsp ground coriander
1 tsp dried mint
¼ tsp smoked paprika
¼ tsp chilli flakes
4 large tomatoes,
    skinned and chopped
    (see page 224)
1 pomegranate
handful of mint leaves,
    shredded
salt and black pepper

Aubergines are great vessels for stuffing. We've given the lamb a Middle Eastern-style spicing and have served it sprinkled with almonds, mint and pomegranate, though you can leave out the pomegranate if you can't find any. Good with couscous, a leafy side salad or wilted spinach.

Heat the oven to 220°C/Gas 7. Cut the aubergine in half lengthways. Score the flesh in a criss-cross pattern. Drizzle liberally with oil and season with salt and pepper. Place skin-side up in a baking dish. Bake for 45 minutes or until the flesh is soft and tender right the way through.

Meanwhile, put the almonds in a dry frying pan. Heat gently, stirring, until golden. Remove to a plate and keep to one side.

Heat 2 tablespoons of oil in a frying pan. Add the onion and fry on a low heat, stirring, for 10 minutes.

Add the lamb and fry, stirring, on a medium heat to brown. Add the garlic, cumin coriander, dried mint, smoked paprika and chilli flakes and stir for 2 minutes. Add the chopped tomatoes. Season and simmer for 30 minutes, adding a splash of water if needed to stop the meat drying out.

Cut the pomegranate in half crossways. Take a rolling pin or the handle of a wooden spoon. Hold the pomegranate cut-side down in your hand over a bowl and bash the skin; the seeds will fall out (most of them anyway). Pick out any pith that does fall in; there shouldn't be much with this technique, but it tastes bitter, so remove any you find.

Once the aubergine flesh is tender, remove it from the oven. Carefully scoop out as much of the flesh as you can, keeping the aubergine skins intact. Add the flesh to the lamb. Stir and simmer for 5 minutes. Check the seasoning. Spoon the lamb mixture into the aubergine skins. Sprinkle over the almonds, pomegranate seeds and mint to serve.

may to july
broad beans

Broad beans are the only beans that are truly happy in our damp, cool climate; so much so that the first sowings can be made in late October or November, though a February sowing often produces a better crop and only a week or two later. The first flowers appear in April, releasing a gorgeous scent to draw in the few bees that are hardy enough to venture out.

Like many children, I dreaded the dry furriness of broad beans. In my middle years, however, the smell of them makes my heart skip a beat and I look forward to their brief season. I am lucky enough to be able to pick plentiful young beans and enjoy them fingernail size, raw in salads, perhaps with a few pecorino shavings. I keep the double-podding – a pleasing task but time-consuming – for later in the season when the beans are getting hard, pale and much larger. I also like a less time-consuming option for mature beans – boiling then mashing them and putting them through a coarse mouli (if you have one) to make a hummus-style paste with a combination of some or all of: olive oil, garlic, mint and paprika or chilli.

Guy

broad beans

storage

Broad beans keep well in their pods in the salad drawer at the bottom of the fridge and they should stay fresh for a week, even if the pods wilt a little.

prep

Broad beans have two layers of protection: the outer pod and the individual inner skin. The smallest, youngest beans definitely need only the outer pod removing before cooking. With larger broad beans, there is much debate about 'double-podding' (removing the skins as well). Some cooks can't see the point – the skins add their own flavour and it's quicker and less wasteful not to bother. Others insist that double-podding is worth it, giving beans that are brighter green, sweeter tasting and more tender. We'll leave it up to you, but if you're not usually a fan of broad beans, double-podding might convert you. To shell, just split the pod open along its seam and squeeze out the bean. The pods can be composted.

HOW MUCH DO YOU NEED?

For 300g of podded/shelled broad beans, you will need around 900g of bean pods. Mixed with other ingredients, such as in a pasta or rice dish, 200–300g of podded beans should be enough for two to four people, depending on the dish.

eating broad beans raw

The smallest beans, around 1cm long, can be eaten raw just as they are. Try them in a salad with fresh mint, lemon juice and crispy bacon, crumbled feta or grilled halloumi. Or eat them straight from their pods as a snack with pecorino cheese, as they do in Italy.

cooking

Nine times out of ten, we just briefly blanch beans, then add them to the dish we're making, be it a salad, pasta dish, rice dish, vegetable ragout or dip.

blanch and refresh

Bring a saucepan of salted water to a rolling boil. Add the beans and boil for just 2–3 minutes. Start testing after a couple of minutes, or even a minute if they're small. As soon as the chalkiness is gone, they are done. Lift out with a strainer or slotted spoon and eat immediately while hot, or plunge into ice-cold water to stop the cooking and fix the colour. Drain once completely cooled. If you are double-podding (see above), do it now. Keep the skinned beans cold to maintain their vibrant colour.

IDEAS FOR USING BLANCHED BROAD BEANS

* Toss with other summery green vegetables to make a salad. Dress with lemon juice and olive oil and finish with torn mint leaves and something savoury, such as bacon, prosciutto, feta, grilled halloumi or shavings of pecorino or Parmesan. For extra body, add some couscous or bulghur wheat.

* Reheat in olive oil with crushed garlic and perhaps a sprig of rosemary. For extra depth of flavour, first fry some diced onions and pancetta, prosciutto or Serrano ham, then add the beans. Serve solo or toss with gnocchi or pasta along with Parmesan and black pepper.

* Add to a plain risotto five minutes before the end of cooking (see page 37 for the basic risotto recipe).

* Fold into cooked rice, quinoa, couscous or bulghur wheat along with plenty of chopped dill, parsley, coriander and chives.

* Smash in a mortar with chopped garlic, lemon juice, olive oil and dill or mint. Use as a dip for pitta bread or spread on to bruschetta. For a creamy dip, mix in crème fraîche, yoghurt, ricotta or smashed feta. Dips and spreads are good for bigger and older beans, which tend to be less sweet.

griddled/roasted in their outer pods

Whole broad beans can be griddled
or roasted; the beans cook inside their
protective pods and the work of podding
is left to the diner. If the pods are tender
enough, you can eat them too.

TO GRILL Light the barbecue or heat a
cast-iron griddle pan. Toss the whole beans
with olive oil and salt and grill for about
5 minutes, turning occasionally, until wilted
and charred. Test one to see if the beans
inside have cooked; if they're still chalky,
give them a few more minutes. Serve as they
are or scattered with fresh herbs, chilli flakes,
lemon zest and lemon wedges to squeeze.

TO ROAST Toss the pods with olive oil and
salt, spread on a baking sheet and roast in
an oven heated to 220°C/Gas 7 for 20–30
minutes. Serve as above.

work well with...

* Cheese – feta, goat's cheese, halloumi,
  mozzarella, Parmesan, pecorino, ricotta
* Starches – bulghur, couscous, gnocchi,
  pasta, potatoes, rice
* Herbs – especially dill, mint, rosemary,
  summer savory
* Lamb
* Lemon
* Pork – bacon, chorizo, pancetta,
  prosciutto, Serrano ham, roast pork

broad bean, quinoa, watercress and sheep's cheese

quick & easy

vegetarian (if you use vegetarian cheese)

SERVES 4

100g quinoa
250–300g podded broad
    beans (approximately
    750–900g in their pods)
4 spring onions, finely sliced
3 tbsp olive oil, more to taste
juice of 1 lemon,
    more to taste
2 tbsp chopped mint leaves
2 tbsp chopped dill
100g watercress, washed,
    any particularly large
    stalks removed
100g sheep's cheese,
    crumbled

We try to sell at least a couple of sheep's cheeses alongside our veg boxes. The tangy, feta-style Wootton White from Wootton Dairy in Somerset or the soft, fresh-tasting Sussex Slipcote from High Weald Dairy in Sussex are both great for crumbling over salads. If you can buy the multi-coloured quinoa, which has the white, red and black grains, it adds a nuttier flavour. This makes a very good packed lunch.

Bring a large pan of water to the boil. Rinse the quinoa in a sieve under cold water, then add to the pan. Cook for 13–14 minutes, until just tender but with some bite. Drain and allow to cool.

In another pan of boiling water, boil the broad beans for 3 minutes, then drain and refresh in a bowl of cold water. Remove the outer skins, if you wish, to reveal the bright green beans. Toss with the quinoa, spring onions, olive oil, lemon juice, mint and dill. Season with salt and pepper and add more lemon juice and/or olive oil to taste, if needed. Serve on a bed of watercress and crumble over the sheep's cheese.

VARIATIONS
* Try goat's instead of sheep's cheese.
* Replace the quinoa with a tin of white beans, or couscous or bulghur wheat.
* Use sugar snap peas instead of broad beans.
* Add a handful of mixed seeds for extra nutrients and a bit of crunch.

broad bean and rocket pappardelle

quick & easy

vegetarian (if you use
a vegetarian alternative
to Parmesan)

Don't let the fancy name or the quantity of butter put you off
this simple pasta sauce: a classic French beurre blanc is is basically
just a lot of butter whisked into a little wine - delicious as a bit
of a treat.

**SERVES 4 AS A MAIN
OR 6 AS A STARTER**

300g podded broad beans
(approximately 900g
in their pods)
300g dried pappardelle
or tagliatelle egg pasta
6 tbsp dry white wine
2 tbsp white wine vinegar
200g unsalted butter, cut
into 2cm cubes and left
at room temperature
50g Parmesan, finely grated
4 good handfuls of rocket
leaves, washed and dried
2 or 3 squeezes of
lemon juice
salt and pepper

Blanch the beans in boiling water until one easily pops out of
its skin when squeezed, about a minute. Drain and immediately
refresh the beans in ice-cold water. Squeeze the beans out of
their skins and set aside.

Bring a large pan of well-salted water to a boil, and cook the
pasta according to the packet instructions, until al dente.

Meanwhile, in a small saucepan, boil the wine and vinegar
until only 2 tablespoons of liquid remains (it's easy to go too far,
so watch closely.) Remove the pan from the heat and whisk in two
cubes of butter. Return to a low heat and whisk in the remaining
butter, one cube at a time. Ensure the mixture does not come
anywhere near boiling. It should be a hot, thickened, creamy,
sauce. When all but the last couple of cubes of butter have been
whisked in, taste and decide if you need the remaining butter or
not. It should taste buttery with some acidity, but not too much.
Season well. Leave somewhere warm, whisking occasionally.

Drain the pasta, reserving a few tablespoons of its cooking water.
Return to the pan and stir in the butter sauce, beans, Parmesan,
half the rocket, a few tablespoons of reserved cooking liquid to
loosen if needed, a couple of squeezes of lemon juice and black
pepper. Cook over a very low heat for a minute, stirring gently, just
to wilt the rocket. Taste and add more seasoning or lemon juice if
needed. Serve immediately, garnished with the remaining rocket.

VARIATION
* Try this with French beans or blanched and chopped spinach
or chard leaves.

beans, pods and cured ham (*habas con jamón*)

long slow cook

SERVES 4

1 onion, finely sliced
4 tbsp olive oil
1kg young broad beans
    in their pods, or 1kg
    podded older beans
70g sliced cured ham,
    or streaky bacon or
    pancetta, diced
2 garlic cloves, chopped
200ml dry white wine
    or sherry, or a mix
    of the two
200ml water or light
    chicken stock
handful of parsley, chopped
salt and black pepper

Thrifty - by virtue of using the pods - and tasty too. Unlike most broad bean recipes, here the beans are cooked slowly to break down the pods, resulting in a rich, winey and earthy stew with a green/grey colour. We were apprehensive when we first came across a version of this Spanish classic in Elisabeth Luard's epic tome *European Peasant Cookery*, but it is worth the wait.

Fry the onion in the olive oil over a low heat until starting to soften, about 8 minutes. If you are using bean pods, top-and-tail them and, using a vegetable peeler, remove any stringy bits from both sides of the pods. Slice the pods into short, bean-sized chunks – you can be fairly rustic with this.

Add the ham and garlic to the onions and fry gently for 5 minutes. Tip in the beans, followed by the wine and water or stock. Bring up to a simmer and stir in the parsley.

Simmer on a low heat with a loose-fitting lid for at least an hour, or until the pods are soft and tender. Add a dash more liquid if it looks as if it is drying out. Check the seasoning at the end and add some salt and pepper if it needs it.

VARIATIONS
* Add a bit of green to the dish towards the end of the cooking time. Throw in some finely sliced green beans, some wilted chopped spinach or spring greens, add a handful of peas, or all of the above.
* Stir in a large spoonful of chunky tomato sauce or some chopped tomatoes.
* Serve this dish as a hearty gratin by adding a dash of cream, putting it in a shallow baking dish and covering in fresh sourdough breadcrumbs blended with a little olive oil. Bake at 180°C/Gas 4 for 15 minutes until the breadcrumbs are golden.

broad bean, saffron and new potato salad

quick & easy

vegan

This warm salad combines two of the best veg Britain has to offer at this time of year. The bright red saffron threads add a wonderful colour and subtle flavour but use it sparingly, or the flavour can be cloying. Try using a small handful of chervil for a slightly different flavour to parsley, or alternatively some chopped chives.

SERVES 4

800g new potatoes,
    scrubbed clean and
    cut in halves, or
    quarters if large
good pinch of
    saffron threads
200g podded broad beans
    (approximately 600g
    in their pods)
4 tbsp olive oil
2 tbsp chopped parsley leaves
juice of ½ lemon (to taste)
salt and pepper

Put the potatoes in a saucepan and add just enough water to cover them, along with a good pinch of salt. Bring to the boil and cook for 12–15 minutes, until tender. Once the water comes to the boil, put the saffron threads in a large bowl and add 1 tablespoon of the boiling water. Leave the saffron to steep.

While the potatoes are cooking, bring another pan of water to the boil. Add the podded beans to the pan and boil for 3 minutes. Drain and refresh in a bowl of cold water, then drain again.

If the beans are large, you might want to double-pod them, but there's no need to do so if they're small and the skins are tender.

Once the potatoes are cooked, drain and toss them in the saffron liquid. Leave to cool. Add the broad beans. Toss in the olive oil and parsley and add salt, pepper and lemon juice to taste.

VARIATIONS
This will work with other beans or peas too. Or try tossing in some cooked, shredded spring or summer greens, spinach or chard leaves.

crushed broad bean bruschetta

quick & easy

vegetarian (if you use
vegetarian cheese)

This makes a great sharing plate for a party or barbecue and the recipe can easily be scaled up to serve more. To get ahead, boil and mash the beans and keep in the fridge, toast the bread just before your guests arrive then mix the cheese, mint, chilli and oil with the beans just before serving.

SERVES 4 AS A STARTER

600g young broad beans
   in their pods
1 lemon
4 tbsp olive oil, plus a little
   more for drizzling
2 tbsp grated Parmesan
   or vegetarian equivalent,
   plus more to serve
2 tbsp finely chopped
   mint leaves
pinch of dried chilli flakes
thin slices of sourdough
   or ciabatta
1 garlic clove

Boil the beans in salted water for 3 minutes until tender, double-pod, then mash roughly with a fork. Finely zest the lemon, then squeeze the juice of one half into the beans. Stir in the olive oil, lemon zest, Parmesan, mint and chilli. Season with salt and pepper to taste (you may want a little more lemon juice too).

Toast, grill or griddle the bread, then rub with a cut clove of garlic. Drizzle with some olive oil, then pile on the broad bean mixture and grate over a little more Parmesan to serve.

broad bean fritters

quick & easy

vegetarian (if you use
vegetarian cheese)

These simple fritters make a good vegetarian main course but
you could also serve smaller ones as starters or canapés for a
summer party (they can be made in advance and gently warmed
through in a low oven). Kids generally love them, particularly
the dinky-sized ones.

SERVES 4

300g podded broad beans
    (approximately
    900g in their pods)
125g self-raising flour
2 large eggs
2 tbsp crème fraîche
125ml milk
200g soft, mild sheep's or
    goat's cheese, crumbled
small handful of mint
    leaves, chopped
small handful of chives,
    snipped or chopped
a little sunflower or olive oil
    and a knob of butter,
    for frying
sweet chilli sauce,
    to serve (optional)

Cook the beans in a pan of boiling water for 3 minutes, then
drain and refresh in cold water. Peel off the outer skins and
discard, leaving the bright green inner bean. In a large bowl,
whisk the flour, eggs, crème fraîche and milk until you have a
smooth, thick batter. Crumble in the cheese. Stir in the broad
beans, mint and chives and season with salt and pepper.

Melt a little oil and butter in a large frying pan. Add spoonfuls
of the mixture (you'll need to cook in two or three batches) and
cook on a medium heat for 2–3 minutes, until golden brown on
the bottom (you'll see small bubbles appearing from underneath
as they're ready). Flip and cook for 2 minutes or so on the other
side, until cooked through. Serve with sweet chilli sauce for
dipping, if you like.

VARIATIONS
* Use a gluten-free self-raising flour if you prefer.
* Use chopped up French or sliced runner beans instead
of broad beans.
* Vary the cheese – try a saltier feta-style sheep's cheese.

june to september

cour-
gettes

A freshly picked courgette is a delight and needs little cooking or embellishment. Unfortunately courgettes are too often held in a cold room for two or three weeks without loss of appearance, by which time they taste of nothing and will have lost most of their nutritive value.

We plant our courgettes under fleece in late April and expect to start picking in late June. In a decent summer, by early July they are growing so fast that they have to be picked daily. By late July we are buried in them and almost willing the arrival of mildew, which reduces leaf area and normally brings the crop to its knees by the end of August.

Baby courgettes are pretty tasteless and have happily fallen out of fashion; yellow courgettes also lack any culinary merit and are best avoided, but a stuffed, deep-fried courgette flower can be a wonderful thing, and the flowers also add an impressive finish to salads. Sadly we can't send them out in the boxes - we've learned the hard way that the flowers don't travel well - but if you grow your own then don't waste them.

Guy

courgettes

storage

Keep courgettes in the salad drawer of the fridge and use within a week. They're much nicer when fresh and firm; they lose their sweetness as they age.

prep

There's no need to peel courgettes – just wash them and trim a little off each end. They can be sliced, diced, grated, cut into batons or strips, or spiralised, the latest craze for vegetables, which is great for getting kids to try them. Overgrown specimens may have spongy insides, in which case remove their seedy cores – we'll try not to send you these!

WHEN TO SALT COURGETTES

Courgettes hold a lot of water so it's a good idea to salt them before using them in a pickle or chutney recipe, or if you want them to hold their shape during slow-cooking. Chop as desired, then toss with a very generous sprinkling of salt and leave in a colander set over a bowl for 2 or 3 hours. Rinse in cold water and pat dry before using. It's also better to salt grated courgettes before frying, for example in fritters. Grated courgette only needs to be left for half an hour. Rinse and squeeze well to extract as much water as possible. If you're short of time, put unsalted grated courgette in a clean tea towel and wring out as much excess moisture as you can.

eating courgettes raw

Fresh, young courgettes are succulent raw. Slice them crossways very thinly (with a mandolin if you have one) or use a vegetable peeler to pare off long ribbons. Toss with olive oil, lemon juice, salt and fresh herbs (see page 77).

cooking

Courgettes respond well to frying, roasting, grilling, baking and braising – there's (almost) nothing you can't do with them. And if you want yet more ways to cook your courgettes, try grating and baking them in a cake (see page 86); they work much like carrots, adding moisture and a very mild flavour.

grill/griddle

Slice the courgettes lengthways, no more than 5mm thick. Rub the slices with olive oil and salt and grill either on the barbecue, on a pre-heated cast-iron griddle pan on the stove, or on a baking sheet placed about 8cm beneath the oven grill. Make sure that the heat is only moderately high otherwise they'll burn before cooking through. They will need 3–4 minutes on each side, depending on their thickness.

HOW TO USE GRILLED COURGETTE IN SALAD

* Keep it green and mix with blanched green beans or grilled asparagus, baby spinach leaves and a lemon basil dressing.

* Bulk it out with tinned white beans and add colour with roasted cherry tomatoes or chopped sun-dried tomatoes.

* Layer with cooked Puy lentils, crumbled feta, torn mint and a balsamic dressing.

* Keep it simple and eat dressed with a little crushed garlic, a squeeze of lemon and some torn mint or basil.

* Dress with Asian flavours such as soy sauce, toasted sesame seeds and sliced spring onions. You could also make a glaze with roughly equal quantities of miso, honey, soy sauce and rice wine vinegar and brush this over freshly grilled courgettes. This is also good with grilled aubergines (see page 47).

* For a Mediterranean sandwich, stuff pittas or ciabatta with courgette, mozzarella, fresh basil and black olive tapenade.

* Roll up long slices of grilled courgette around cubes of feta and secure with a toothpick, or spread them with ricotta and roll up – some chopped dill also works well here.

courgettes

fry

Courgettes can be quick-, slow- or deep-fried, all to good effect. Grated courgettes also make good fritters (see our recipe on page 82).

QUICK-FRY Slice thinly and fry in a glug of oil over a moderate heat, stirring frequently until just wilted – about 5 minutes. For extra flavour, add some finely chopped, grated or crushed garlic at the start, and finish with a few chilli flakes and a handful of chopped herbs (see page 77).

For an Indian dal, fry garlic, chilli and ground cumin in butter for a couple of minutes, then add the sliced courgettes and cook for a few minutes more. Fold them into cooked red lentils or split mung beans mixed with grated ginger and turmeric.

Courgettes are also great to stir-fry: heat sunflower or peanut oil in a wok, stir-fry some minced garlic, grated ginger and chilli for a few seconds then add the courgettes, cut into matchsticks along with any other summer veg. Fry over high heat, tossing frequently, until tender, a matter of minutes, then finish with soy sauce and sesame oil. Eat with noodles or rice.

SLOW-FRY Slice the courgettes into rounds of about 1 cm thick or cut them into batons. Heat some oil in a pan and then slowly fry the courgettes over a low heat until meltingly tender and nicely caramelised around the outside, about 20–25 minutes. Use a wide pan so you don't crowd the courgettes. If you want to add chopped garlic and/or chilli, do it when the courgettes are at least half cooked so they don't burn. Slow-fried courgettes are fantastic with pasta, along with a squeeze of lemon juice and plenty of grated Parmesan.

DEEP-FRY Like aubergines, courgettes deep-fry better if pre-salted: cut them into cubes or batons and salt as described on page 46, then deep-fry them. Heat a deep fat fryer with oil to 180°C. Keeping a constant eye on the temperature, fry the courgettes in batches without overcrowding until golden on the outside and tender within. Remove with a slotted spoon to kitchen paper to soak up the excess oil, and sprinkle with salt.

simmer

Braise chunks or batons of courgette slowly in a little water or stock (they should be about half submerged) for around half an hour. They might seem about to disintegrate, but their skin will hold them together if kept at a low simmer. Spice them up with onions, garlic, ginger and curry powder, or add Mexican flavours with smoked paprika, oregano, cumin and a tin of kidney or black beans, or some sweetcorn kernels.

If you have a glut, make courgette soup: slowly fry onions and garlic first, add evenly sliced or cubed courgettes and just enough water or stock to cover, then simmer until tender. Blitz smooth and finish with a swirl of cream and a handful of chopped herbs and/or crumbled Stilton.

Courgettes pair well with other veg in soup – try potatoes, peas, watercress, rocket or wild garlic, or see our recipe for Corn and Courgette Soup on page 215, or our Tomato and Courgette Pasta bowl on page 236.

roast

Cut courgettes into chunks or quarter them lengthways, toss with oil and salt and spread over a lined baking sheet. Cook in a hot oven (around 200°C/Gas 6) for 20–30 minutes. They're done when completely tender and starting to colour. Eat as they are, combined with other roast summer veg such as aubergines and peppers, or see our ideas on how to use grilled courgette on page 75 for further inspiration.

bake

Stuffing courgettes is more work than other cooking methods but makes a complete meal. Cut courgettes in half lengthways, scoop out the seedy insides, rub with oil and salt and bake in an oven heated to 200°C/Gas 6, for 20 minutes. Meanwhile, make a stuffing by mixing together fried onions, the diced courgette flesh and anything else you fancy (e.g. minced lamb or sausage meat, cooked quinoa, breadcrumbs, chopped olives, grated cheese, chopped herbs). Stuff the courgettes without packing them too firmly, and return them to the oven for another 20 minutes or so, until the stuffing is golden.

Sliced courgettes also work well on pizzas and open tarts, or substitute courgettes for the tomatoes in the recipe for Tomato and Gruyère Galette on page 233.

work well with...

* Cheese – blue cheese, feta, goat's cheese, halloumi, mozzarella, Parmesan, ricotta
* Chilli
* Herbs – especially basil, coriander, dill, mint
* Indian or Mexican spices
* Lamb
* Lemon
* Mediterranean flavours – anchovies, capers, garlic, olives, pine nuts
* Mediterranean-style veg – aubergine, peppers, red onion
* Peppery leaves – mustard leaves, rocket, watercress
* Pork – especially bacon and pancetta
* Tomatoes

fried courgette and mint salad

easy

vegan

This marinated salad works well as part of a Mediterranean-style spread of dishes or mix it with cooked lentils, quinoa or beans to make a simple main or lunchbox meal. If you're short of time, just fry the courgettes without salting them, using slightly less vinegar as it won't have time to meld with the courgettes.

SERVES 4

450g small courgettes
3 tbsp extra virgin olive oil
2 garlic cloves, sliced
1½ tbsp red wine vinegar
small bunch of mint
   leaves, chopped
salt and black pepper

Trim the ends off the courgettes. If they're thin, cut them in half lengthways, if fatter, quarter them, then cut into 5cm lengths.

Arrange the courgettes in one layer in a colander, sprinkle with salt, and leave for 30 minutes to 1 hour. Rinse and pat dry.

Fry the courgettes briskly in the olive oil with the sliced garlic until browned and tender, no more than 5 minutes.

Tip the fried courgettes into a shallow dish, drizzle over the wine vinegar, scatter over the mint, season with salt and pepper and stir. Leave to marinate for a couple of hours before serving.

VARIATIONS
* Crumble over a salty sheep's cheese to serve.
* Add a little chopped fresh chilli or some dried chilli flakes.

courgette kuku

quick & easy

vegetarian

SERVES 4

3 tbsp sunflower or
    light olive oil
1 red or white onion,
    finely chopped
500g courgettes,
    cut into 5mm slices
2 garlic cloves, finely
    chopped, grated
    or crushed
6 large eggs, lightly beaten
100ml milk
handful of chives, chopped
handful of mint, chopped
handful of dill, chopped
large handful of flat-leaf
    parsley, chopped
salt and pepper

For the advieh spice blend
¼ tsp each of ground
    turmeric, nutmeg,
    ground ginger and
½ tsp each ground cumin
    and ground coriander

A Persian version of a set omelette, similar to a frittata, kuku uses a mixed spice blend called advieh, which can vary a lot, so allow yourself free rein. If you can, use whole spices ground in a coffee grinder or a pestle and mortar. A traditional kuku is mostly made up of chopped fresh herbs. We've given a rough amount, but really add as many herbs as you can cram in! All egg dishes such as flans, frittata and tortillas are best served not straightaway, but just warm or at room temperature. Serve with a simple green salad.

Mix all the spices for the advieh blend together in a small bowl.

Heat 2 tablespoons of the oil in a large heavy-bottomed frying pan. Add the onion and fry on a low heat for 10 minutes to soften, stirring now and then.

Heat the grill to medium.

Remove the onion to a plate and add the remaining tablespoon of oil to the pan. Turn the heat up, add the courgettes and fry (in batches if need be) until they have some colour, about 2–3 minutes per side. Add the garlic, advieh spice mix and onion. Fry for a further 2 minutes, stirring, then season with salt and pepper.

Whisk the eggs with the milk in a large bowl, stir in the herbs and pour over the top of the courgettes. Cook very gently for a few minutes until just set on the bottom. Finish under the grill until just set all the way through (test by gently tipping it sideways, no runny egg should appear). Wait for at least 5 minutes before cutting into wedges to serve.

VARIATIONS
* Add blanched and chopped spinach or chard leaves instead of, or as well as, the courgette, or some roasted chunks of aubergine.
* Instead of making the advieh mix, use 1 tablespoon of mild or medium curry powder.

spiced courgette and chickpea fritters with tomato, cucumber and mint salsa

quick & easy

vegetarian

Most people think of basil being the herb match for tomatoes, but mint works really well too. You could also try other grated veg in this; squash in autumn or carrot in the winter work well, served with a seasonal chutney instead of a fresh salsa.

SERVES 4

500g courgettes, grated
1 x 400g tin chickpeas, rinsed and drained
3 spring onions, finely sliced
1 green chilli, deseeded and finely chopped
3 tbsp chopped coriander leaves
100g gram (chickpea) flour
1 tbsp curry powder
1 tsp peeled and finely grated fresh ginger
finely grated zest of 1 lime
240g plain yoghurt
sunflower or light olive oil, for frying

For the salsa
5–6 tomatoes, depending on size, deseeded and chopped
1 small or 1/2 large cucumber, finely diced
small bunch of mint, leaves finely shredded
1 or 2 chillies, finely chopped
2 tbsp extra virgin olive oil
juice of 1/2 lime, plus more to taste (or lemon juice)
salt and black pepper

Put a clean tea towel in a colander over a bowl. Tip in the grated courgettes. Wring the towel several times, to squeeze out as much moisture as you can. Wash and dry the bowl.

Tip the chickpeas into the bowl and lightly mash with a fork, so some are crushed and some whole. Add the courgettes, spring onion, chilli, coriander, gram flour, curry powder, ginger and 1/2 teaspoon of salt and mix together well. Cover and chill for at least 30 minutes.

Meanwhile, make the salsa: mix all the ingredients in a bowl, season and leave to stand. Mix the lime zest into the yoghurt.

Roughly shape the courgette mixture into eight balls, then flatten into pattie/burger shapes. Heat a thin layer of oil in a large non-stick frying pan. Fry the patties in batches, on a medium heat for about 3–4 minutes on each side, until golden. Drain on kitchen paper. If cooking in batches, keep the cooked fritters warm in a low oven while you make the rest.

Serve the fritters with a dollop of yoghurt and the salsa on the side.

VARIATION
If you want to make these for kids, and prefer them not to be too spicy, leave out the chilli, add just half the amount of curry powder or leave it out completely and add dried mint (1/2 teaspoon or so).

courgette, chickpea and coconut curry

quick & easy

vegan

Use a teaspoon rather than a knife or peeler to scrape the skin off your ginger - it avoids wastage. Cheap teaspoons have sharper edges and work better than posh cutlery. Serve this curry with plain boiled basmati rice and a good dollop of yoghurt.

SERVES 2

2 tbsp sunflower or light
   olive, for frying
1 onion, finely chopped
$\frac{1}{2}$ tsp black mustard seeds
$\frac{1}{2}$ tsp ground cumin
$\frac{1}{2}$ tsp ground coriander
$\frac{1}{4}$ tsp ground turmeric
1 chilli, deseeded and finely
   chopped (leave the seeds
   in for more heat)
2 garlic cloves, finely
   chopped, grated
   or crushed
4cm piece of fresh ginger,
   peeled and finely grated
1 tbsp tomato purée
1 x 400g tin coconut milk
1 cinnamon stick
$\frac{1}{2}$ x 400g tin cooked
   chickpeas, drained
   and rinsed
2 large courgettes, cut in
   half lengthways, then
   into bite-sized pieces
2 tomatoes, roughly diced
squeeze of lime juice
large handful of coriander,
   roughly chopped
salt and black pepper

Heat 2 tablespoons of oil in a large pan and add the onion. Fry on a very low heat, stirring now and then, until the onion is soft and translucent, without colouring, about 10 minutes.

Add the mustard seeds, cumin, coriander, turmeric and chilli. Fry until you hear the mustard seeds starting to pop. Add the garlic, ginger and tomato purée and fry, stirring, for 2 minutes.

Give the coconut milk a quick stir then add to the onions with the cinnamon stick. Bring to a simmer, cover and cook for 10 minutes to infuse the coconut milk with the spices.

Add the chickpeas, courgettes and tomatoes, then cover the pan and cook for approx. 8–10 minutes, until the courgettes are tender.

Remove the cinnamon stick, add a squeeze of lime juice and season to taste, then stir in the chopped coriander.

VARIATION
It will take a little longer for them to soften, you might need a little more liquid too, but try with chunks of aubergine or sweet potato.

courgette and halloumi kebabs
with green tahini dressing

quick & easy

vegetarian (if you use
vegetarian halloumi)

A great vegetarian option for a barbecue or a simple summery lunch. Stir lemon zest, toasted, flaked almonds or chopped pistachios through a bowl of couscous to serve alongside, or just griddle or roast some red peppers (see page 160).

3 large or 4 smaller
    courgettes, chopped into
    large bite-sized pieces
300g halloumi, cut into
    large cubes
2 green chillies, deseeded
    and finely chopped
4 tbsp sunflower or light
    olive oil

For the dressing
2 tbsp light tahini
2 tbsp yoghurt
1 garlic clove, crushed
2 tbsp olive oil
juice of ½ a lemon
    (more to taste)
handful of coriander leaves,
    finely chopped
handful of mint leaves,
    finely chopped
salt and black pepper

If you are using wooden or bamboo skewers rather than metal ones, soak them in cold water for 20 minutes to stop them burning when they cook.

To make the dressing, stir the tahini with the yoghurt until you have a smooth paste. Whisk in the garlic, olive oil and lemon juice and add water, a little at a time, until the dressing has the consistency of pouring cream. Stir in the chopped herbs. Season to taste with salt, pepper and more lemon juice.

Thread the courgettes and halloumi on to the skewers. Mix the chillies with 4 tablespoons of oil. Brush a little of this over the kebabs.

Heat a griddle or non-stick frying pan (or use the barbecue). Fry the kebabs, brushing them with more chilli oil and turning them carefully every few minutes, until the courgettes and halloumi are golden brown. Serve with the tahini dressing alongside to drizzle over the kebabs.

VARIATIONS
* Try chunks of pepper or quartered mushrooms instead of, or as well as, the courgette.
* Drizzle with a cucumber, mint and yoghurt sauce like tzatziki (see page 90) instead of the tahini.

courgette, lemon and poppyseed cake

vegetarian

SERVES 12

75ml whole milk
2 tbsp poppy seeds
finely grated zest of 2 lemons
250g unsalted butter,
    plus a little extra for
    greasing the tin
250g soft light brown sugar
4 eggs, separated
½ tsp almond extract
200g gluten-free
    self-raising flour
75g ground almonds
250g grated courgettes
    (about 2 medium)

For the icing
300g icing sugar
1½ tsp finely grated
    lemon zest
30g unsalted butter
1 tbsp poppy seeds
2 tbsp lemon juice

Don't be put off by the idea of vegetables in a cake – think of carrot cake; the courgettes in this lemony-almondy sponge keep it moist. We use gluten-free flour as it absorbs more liquid than ordinary flour and gives the cake the best texture but it will work with regular self-raising flour if that's what you have at home.

Heat the oven to 180°C/Gas 4. Lightly grease a 23cm spring-form cake tin with a little butter and line it with baking parchment.

In a small pan over a low heat, warm the milk with the poppy seeds and lemon zest for a couple of minutes, then set aside to cool.

Cream the butter and sugar in a large bowl until pale, light and fluffy (an electric hand mixer makes life easier). Beat in the egg yolks, one at a time. Gently fold in the almond extract, flour and ground almonds, then fold in the courgettes and cooled milk.

Whisk the egg whites in a separate bowl until they form stiff peaks. Add a large spoon of the egg white to the courgette mixture and stir it in, then gently fold in the rest, keeping in as much air as possible.

Pour the mixture into the tin and bake for about an hour (depending on your oven), until just firm to the touch; the cake should spring back when you lightly press the middle. Cool the cake in the tin for 15 minutes then turn it on to a wire rack to cool completely.

To make the icing, sift the icing sugar into a bowl and stir in the lemon zest. Melt the butter and, working quickly, pour it over the icing sugar. Add the lemon juice and quickly whisk together, adding a splash of hot water if needed, until you have a thick but spreadable icing. Use a palette knife to spread it over the cake. Sprinkle over the poppy seeds and leave for about 30 minutes so the icing can set a little before serving.

cucumbers

Tricky to grow in our climate, most non-organic cucumbers are grown hydroponically, never seeing any soil. I really think you can taste the difference when they are grown in soil. Our Devon crop starts in late spring and can last through to October in a warm year. In winter we resort to our growers in Spain, to avoid using heated glass.

I am a particular fan of our mini cucumbers, which lend themselves to cucumber pickle, a long-standing Watson family favourite. Making this is a bit of a family ritual at the end of the season. The recipe is on our website, and we also offer pickling kits, spices, jar labels and all, when we have a glut. If you are not a pickling enthusiast, you may find the finished article for sale on our website when my brother Ben makes a batch in our farm kitchen.

Guy

cucumbers

storage

Keep cucumbers in the salad drawer of the fridge. They'll last a week or so, but are best eaten as soon as possible.

prep

You can eat our cucumbers as they are – there's no need to peel. To avoid the cucumber giving off lots of water, especially if it's being left to sit for a while, you can halve it lengthways and use a teaspoon to scoop out the watery, seedy section before chopping. Alternatively, or in addition, salt the sliced cucumber before using it (see below).

ideas for raw cucumber

* Marinate for half an hour with salt, sugar and a little vinegar. Try rice wine vinegar when pairing with Asian dishes.

* Diced small, along with radishes, spring onions and chives, in a creamy dressing (see page 261).

* In a Greek salad, with wedges of ripe tomato, black olives, sliced red onion, chunks of feta, a sprinkling of dried oregano and good olive oil.

* With its cousins, melon or watermelon, crumbled feta and torn mint or basil.

* In tzatziki to go with grilled lamb: mix grated or finely sliced cucumber with thick yoghurt, crushed garlic, a little lemon juice and dried or fresh mint.

* In a quick pickle, ideal for burgers (see pages 94–95).

* Infused in vodka for a refreshing martini. Simply peel and chop cucumber, pour over vodka and leave to infuse for a few days.

* As a summery alternative to lemon in your gin and tonic.

SALTING CUCUMBER

Once cut, cucumbers readily give up their water, resulting in soggy salads. Pre-salting sliced, diced or grated cucumber draws out the excess water, firms up the texture and intensifies the flavour. For pickles, it's an essential step to prevent the excess water diluting the pickling liquid. Layer the prepared cucumber in a colander with a light sprinkling of salt between each layer and leave for 20 minutes, or a couple of hours if making pickle. Water will seep out of the bottom of the colander, so set it inside a bowl. To speed the process, place a plate on top, weighted down. Afterwards, taste a piece: if it's too salty, give the cucumber a quick rinse in cold water, otherwise simply pat or squeeze dry with kitchen paper or a clean tea towel.

cooking

Although it's most often eaten raw, cucumber is actually more versatile than you'd expect and cooking it is an interesting way to change its texture and flavour.

braise

Fry chunks of cucumber in butter, then add stock or cream to barely cover and simmer until the cucumber is tender but still holding its shape, about 5–10 minutes. Season and serve with chicken or fish. For a more elaborate version, fry sliced onions or leeks separately and then add them to the fried cucumber with a little white wine before adding the stock or cream. Finish the dish with chopped dill, chives, parsley or chervil.

fry

In a wok, briefly fry finely chopped garlic, ginger and chilli in very hot vegetable oil, then add thin batons of cucumber and stir-fry until crisp–tender, adding splashes of light soy sauce and rice wine vinegar if you like. Finish with a drizzle of sesame oil and toasted sesame seeds and serve hot or cold.

steam

Peel, deseed and cut the cucumber into chunks or batons then steam over boiling water for just a couple of minutes, then toss in hot melted butter and chopped dill.

grill/griddle

Fire up the barbecue or heat a cast-iron griddle pan. Cut the cucumber into big wedges, fat rounds or slice it lengthways. Rub with oil and then grill for about 5 minutes on each side until nicely charred but still crisp inside. Season, dress with a vinaigrette (see page 260), or simply some lemon juice.

bake

Peel and deseed the cucumber, cut into batons or chunks and pre-salt (see page 90). Toss with a good dose of melted butter or oil, lemon juice or vinegar, salt, pepper and a little sugar, then spread over a roasting tin and bake at 200°C/Gas 6 for about 30 minutes until tender and browned in places, checking halfway through. Finish with a handful of fresh herbs.

work well with...

* Feta cheese or similar
* Herbs – basil, chervil, chives, dill, mint
* Melon and watermelon
* Oily fish – mackerel, salmon
* Shellfish
* Tomatoes
* Vinegar
* Walnuts
* White fish
* Yoghurt and cream

Scandi-style beetroot, potato and cucumber salad

easy

vegetarian

SERVES 4-6

1 bunch of beetroot, approx
    450g, trimmed of leaves,
    left whole in their skins
400g new or waxy salad
    potatoes
1 mini cucumber (or
    ½ standard one), diced
1 apple, cored and diced
2 spring onions or 1 larger
    new season bunched
    onion, finely sliced
2 large or 6 small gherkins,
    finely sliced or diced
    if large
1 bunch of radishes,
    finely sliced (optional)
2 tbsp crème fraîche
2 tbsp yoghurt
2 tbsp chopped dill
2 tbsp chopped parsley
salt and pepper

For a light supper, combine with boiled eggs, rye bread and some green leaves. Or make it part of a picnic.

Boil the beetroot until tender, 30–45 minutes depending on size. (If they're really large, they can take up to an hour or more.) Drain and leave until cool enough to handle, then rub off the skins (they should come away easily). Boil the potatoes for 12–15 minutes, until tender. Drain and leave to cool.

Chop the beetroot and potatoes into bite-sized pieces. Put in a large bowl and add the cucumber, apple, spring onion, gherkins and radish, if using.

In a small bowl, stir together the crème fraîche, yoghurt, dill and parsley. Season with salt and pepper, then gently mix into the veg.

cucumber pickles

These instant pickles are a quick and easy way of spicing up cucumbers. Use the Fiery Thai and Light and Fast pickles immediately – they're not for keeping. The Dark and Spiced version is ready to eat after a couple of hours, and will keep for up to a week in the fridge.

fiery Thai

quick & easy

vegan

SERVES 4

1 large cucumber, peeled, deseeded and thinly sliced (see page 90)
1 tbsp soft light brown sugar (or palm sugar, if you can find it)
juice of 1 lime
1 ½ tsp soy sauce
1 hot red chilli, deseeded and very finely chopped
4 or 5 mint leaves, very finely sliced
leaves from a few basil sprigs, very finely sliced
2 spring onions, very finely sliced
salt

Season the cucumber with a sprinkle of salt. In a large bowl, dissolve the sugar in the lime juice and soy sauce. Add the chilli and cucumber and mix well. Leave to sit for at least 15 minutes.

When ready to serve, add the sliced mint, basil and spring onions and stir through.

light and fast

quick & easy

vegan

SERVES 1
1 large cucumber peeled, deseeded
   and thinly sliced (see page 88)
salt
70g granulated sugar
100ml cider vinegar
3 mint leaves
small handful of dill, finely chopped

Season the cucumber with a little sprinkling of salt.

Put the sugar and vinegar into a small saucepan and heat gently until the sugar has dissolved. Take off the heat, add the mint leaves and allow to cool.

Remove the leaves then pour the cooled liquid over the cucumber and leave for at least 15 minutes.

This keeps well in the fridge for a few days. When ready to serve, remove the cucumber from the liquid and stir in the dill.

dark and spiced

quick & easy

vegan

SERVES 6–8
1 large cucumber, peeled, deseeded
   and thinly sliced (see page 88)
1 small onion, very finely sliced
100ml cider vinegar
70g soft dark brown sugar
1 tsp yellow mustard seeds
½ tsp nigella seeds
½ tsp coriander seeds
¼ tsp ground turmeric
2 whole cloves
1 bay leaf
salt

Season the cucumber with a sprinkle of salt and leave to sit in a colander for an hour.

Put the remaining ingredients into a small pan and bring to the boil. Reduce the heat and simmer until the sugar has dissolved. Leave to cool for 10 minutes.

Place the cucumber in a clip-top jar or a plastic container and pour the still-warm liquid over. Put on the lid and allow to cool fully.

This pickle will be ready to use after a few hours but will keep for up to a week if stored in the fridge.

crunchy cucumber salad with smoked fish and soured cream

quick & easy

This classic Scandinavian combination of smoked fish, cucumber and dill makes a light summer lunch or dinner. Scale up the quantities for a quick and easy buffet dish.

SERVES 2

½ cucumber
4 radishes
1 small fennel bulb
50g mixed salad leaves
250g hot smoked fish
   (salmon, trout or
   mackerel), flaked

For the dressing
4 tbsp soured cream
½ lemon
2 tbsp olive oil
½ small garlic clove,
  very finely minced
small bunch of dill, chopped
salt

Peel and deseed the cucumber and slice into chunky wedges on an angle. Cut the radishes into eight along their length. Trim the fennel tops away to the bulb and discard the outer layer if it looks tough or dry. Cut into quarters and slice out most of the core, leaving just enough to keep things held together. Cut lengthways into thin wedges.

To make the dressing, in a bowl thin the soured cream with a good squeeze of lemon juice, then slowly whisk in the olive oil. Stir in the garlic then season generously with salt and more lemon juice if you think it needs it. Stir through the dill.

Toss the salad leaves, vegetables and dressing together in a large bowl. Stack on to plates and crumble the fish on top.

iced cucumber and yoghurt soup

quick & easy

vegan

SERVES 4

500ml Greek-style or other
    full-fat plain yoghurt
1 bunch of dill, chopped
10 mint leaves, chopped
1 garlic clove, finely chopped
    or crushed
1 tsp caster sugar
2 tbsp olive oil
1 large or 3 mini cucumbers,
    peeled if the skin is tough
    and cut into 5mm dice
salt and pepper
ice cubes, to serve

If you've not tried one before, you'll be pleasantly surprised by
how good a chilled soup is to eat on a hot day. Serve on its own
or with pitta bread for dunking. This also makes a great packed
lunch, carried in a flask to keep it cool (in this case, leave out
the ice cubes and don't use a flask that has previously contained
strong flavoured liquids).

In a bowl, combine the yoghurt, dill, mint, garlic, sugar and olive
oil. Mix well and add the cucumber. Leave to marinate for 1 hour.

When ready to serve, thin with enough cold water to give the
soup the consistency of double cream. Season with salt and pepper
to taste. Pour into soup bowls and add a few ice cubes to each.

july to september

fennel

Florence fennel, or bulb fennel, is a close relative of anise and shares the family's liquorice tang. Not surprisingly it tends to elicit a love-it or hate-it response. To the haters I would beg you to open your minds and try again; you are missing out. Crunchy raw fennel has a potent aniseed flavour, but cooked fennel is a very different beast – sweet and soft. Try our slow-cooked fennel or fennel gratin; the latter has become a signature dish in our Field Kitchen and has converted many a fennel-hater.

Guy

fennel

storage

Store fennel in the salad drawer of the fridge and it should easily last a week before starting to shrivel. If it has green fronds that you want to use, remove them – the bulb keeps better without. The fronds are a delicious addition to salads, pasta dishes and fish (see page 101).

prep

After washing the fennel bulb, slice off any discoloured base and stems protruding from the top. If the outer layer of the bulb is discoloured or dried out, remove that too, or just give it a quick swipe with a good veg peeler. These trimmings are good for the stockpot, especially for fish stock.

For boiling and braising, wedges work best: quarter the fennel lengthways or, if the bulb is big, divide it into six or eight. Remove some of the tough core from each wedge, leaving behind enough to hold it together.

If you are going to eat it raw, slice the fennel very finely: prepare wedges then slice them crossways as finely as you can with a sharp knife, mandolin or food processor.

For diced fennel, treat the bulb like an onion: halve it lengthways, place the halves face down, and slice them first lengthways then across. It will fall apart into dice.

Cut fennel discolours quickly, so prepare it shortly before you use it, or keep it submerged in a bowl of water acidulated with a good squeeze of lemon juice.

eating fennel raw

Fennel has a strong aniseed flavour and is pleasantly crunchy when raw. It's best very finely sliced, or shaved on a mandolin and used in a citrus-based salad – for example with segments of orange or a lemon dressing. Salads that go with raw, finely sliced fennel:

* Segments of orange (or blood orange) with finely sliced red onion, black olives and a good dose of olive oil. Rocket or watercress add a peppery flavour.

* Celery, tossed with sliced spring onions, lemon juice, olive oil and roughly chopped parsley. Raw sliced artichoke hearts make a good addition, and some shaved Parmesan.

* Sliced pears, layered with watercress, blue cheese and toasted walnuts, drizzled with a balsamic and honey vinaigrette.

cooking

The trick to cooking fennel successfully is to cook it thoroughly; its sweet flavour and soft texture need time. Braises and gratins are our favourite techniques, but it's also good grilled and in fish soups and stews.

braise

Cut the fennel into wedges (see page 100). Heat butter or oil, or a mix of the two, in a wide saucepan over moderate heat and fry the wedges for a few minutes on each side until caramelised. Add enough stock, spiked with lemon juice, dry white wine or dry vermouth, to barely cover the fennel, then cover the pan and simmer gently until the fennel is completely tender, about 30 minutes. Remove the fennel, boil the cooking liquid to reduce it, then return the fennel to the pan and stir to coat with the juice.

KEEP THE FRONDS!

The feathery green fronds topping your fennel bulb can be used in salads, as a garnish or tossed through buttery pasta or potatoes. They're the perfect complement to fish – add them to your poaching broth or stuff them inside the cavity of a fish ready for the oven or grill. Or try one of these ideas:

FENNEL SALT Pound the fronds in a mortar together with rock salt, or whizz them in a (mini) food processor. Spread out to dry in a very low oven for 30 minutes, then store in an airtight container for up to 2 weeks. Use on chicken and fish dishes. Or try this with sugar instead and use immediately in lemony cookies and cakes (the sweet version won't keep).

JUICE Blitz them up with fruit or veg – try apples, carrots and oranges – to make a smoothie.

PESTO Combine the fronds with another herb such as parsley or keep it pure. Blitz or pound with Parmesan, walnuts, crushed garlic, olive oil and a little lemon juice.

fennel

fry

Finely sliced or diced fennel can be fried gently in butter or oil to form the base of a risotto, pasta sauce, soup or stew – rather like an onion. Use a low heat, keep the lid on to trap the moisture and stir every now and then. The fennel should be soft and sweet but not too coloured (this may take about 10 minutes). For extra aniseed punch, include a scattering of coarsely ground fennel seeds.

grill/griddle

Charred fennel pairs well with roast lamb; in a salad scattered with fresh mint, black olives and orange wedges; or simply dressed with lemon juice, lemon zest and Parmesan shavings.

Slice the raw fennel lengthways or cut it into wedges no more than 1cm thick, rub with olive oil and salt and grill on a barbecue or griddle on a cast-iron griddle pan over moderate heat, until tender and branded with marks. Fatter wedges will need to be pre-boiled in salted water for 10 minutes until just tender. Drain them well, then oil and grill or griddle as above. If cooking outside, you may find it easier to thread the boiled fennel wedges onto skewers before barbecuing.

IDEAS FOR FRIED FENNEL

* Make a simple bouillabaisse: fry the fennel with onions, leeks and garlic in plenty of olive oil. Add some tinned or chopped fresh tomatoes, a glass of dry white wine, a dash of Pernod (or other anise-flavoured liqueur), a pinch of saffron threads and a litre or more of fish stock and boil until somewhat reduced. Finally, lower the heat and simmer fish and shellfish of your choice for a few minutes until just cooked through. Serve with crusty bread.

* Make a Sicilian-inspired pasta sauce for spaghetti or other long pasta: add crushed garlic and preserved anchovy fillets to the frying fennel, then fresh or tinned sardine fillets. Simmer together with a dash of dry white wine or water, a pinch of saffron threads, some sultanas and lightly toasted pine nuts. Toss with the pasta and any fennel fronds if you have them.

* Make soup: fry the fennel gently together with onions and butter, and, if you like, other veg, such as carrots or potatoes. Stew gently with the lid on until the veg have released their flavour and softened. Don't let them catch or colour – add a splash of water if necessary. Add chicken or veg stock to cover and simmer until completely tender. Blitz until smooth.

boil and bake

For a very simple dish, boil wedges of fennel in salted water until completely tender, about 20 minutes, then serve anointed with butter and any reserved fennel fronds.

Worth the extra effort, however, is a fennel gratin, which is particularly tasty when combined with potato (waxy ones hold their shape better). The veg can be left in wedges or sliced finely. Either way, pre-cook them on the stove until tender before baking them in the oven: boil wedges in salted water, fry wafer-thin slices gently in butter or simmer sliced fennel and potato in cream. Then drain, arrange in a buttered gratin dish and season with salt and black pepper. Pour over cream or stock, or a mix of the two, to barely cover the fennel. Bake at 190°C/Gas 5 for about 30–45 minutes (depending on whether you went for wedges or slices), until the liquid has bubbled and reduced and the fennel has turned golden brown. If you like, sprinkle over grated Parmesan or another hard cheese about 15 minutes before the gratin is done. For a green veg gratin, see our fennel and chard gratin on page 108.

works well with...

* Apples and pears
* Carrots
* Chicken
* Citrus fruit
* Fish and shellfish
* Lamb
* Nuts – almonds, hazelnuts, pine nuts, walnuts
* Olives
* Parmesan
* Pork

pork and fennel ragù

long slow cook

freezable

SERVES 4

1 large onion, finely diced
2 carrots, peeled and
    finely diced
2 celery sticks, finely diced
1 large or 2 small fennel
    bulbs, finely diced
3 tbsp sunflower or light
    olive oil, for frying
6 pork sausages, outer
    casings removed,
    meat crumbled
1 tbsp fennel seeds
1 tsp dried oregano
2 garlic cloves, finely
    chopped, grated
    or crushed
1 tbsp tomato purée
125ml dry white wine
1 x 400g tin chopped
    tomatoes, or a punnet
    (480–500g) of fresh
    tomatoes, diced
1 bay leaf
1/4 tsp chilli flakes
salt and pepper

Fennel is a good base for soups and slow-cooked dishes, losing its strong pungent aniseed flavour for a softer taste once cooked. A ragù is the Italian word for a meat-based sauce, usually served with pasta, but you could also serve this with cooked polenta or rice. For 4 people use about 400g uncooked pasta.

Fry the onion, carrot, celery and fennel in the oil for 20 minutes, stirring now and then and adding a splash of water, if necessary, to stop it sticking. Add the sausage meat and fry for about 5 minutes to brown it.

Add the fennel seeds, oregano and garlic and fry for 2 minutes, then add the tomato purée and wine. Simmer for 3–4 minutes, or until the wine has been absorbed, then add the tomatoes, bay and chilli flakes. Season with salt and pepper, cover and simmer for 30 minutes, then uncover and simmer for a further 30 minutes. Check the seasoning before serving tossed with fresh pasta.

VARIATIONS

* Use minced pork or lamb instead of sausages. If you have any, add a handful of fresh oregano leaves towards the end of cooking.
* Keep any feathery bright green fennel fronds if you have any still attached to the fennel bulb and throw them over the pasta to serve.

fish, fennel and tomatoes in a bag

quick & easy

2 x 150g firm white fish
   fillets (at least 2.5cm thick),
   skinned (ask your
   fishmonger for sustainably
   caught fish)
1 small fennel bulb, trimmed
   and thinly sliced, with any
   green fronds reserved
2 medium tomatoes,
   sliced, or 10 cherry
   tomatoes, halved
2 bay leaves
2 thyme sprigs
2 orange slices
   (or lemon if you prefer)
75ml dry white wine
olive oil
salt and pepper

This a clean and fast way of cooking fish and there's an element of theatre to opening the bag at the table like a crisp packet and getting a nostrilful of fragrance. To make it into a more substantial meal, add a few cooked haricot or cannellini beans or some sliced parboiled new potatoes to the bags.

Heat the oven to 200°C/Gas 6.

First make your bag: if you're using foil, take 2 large squares, fold each in half, and then roll over three sides to form a packet with an opening at the top. If you're using baking parchment, do the same but secure the sides with a couple of staples or it may unfurl as the steam builds up.

Lightly season the fish on both sides.

Toss the fennel and tomatoes together in a bowl with some salt, pepper and a generous slosh of olive oil. Divide evenly between the two bags. Pop a bay leaf, thyme sprig, orange slice and some fennel fronds in each bag and gently sit the fish on top. Divide the wine between the bags and seal the open edge with a few firm turns or staples.

Put the two bags in a roasting tin and bake for about 20 minutes. Serve in the bags – rip open and tuck in.

courgette, fennel and kohlrabi salad

quick & easy

vegan

Riverford Cook Anna is a big fan of using courgettes, fennel and kohlrabi raw, so this simple salad pairs the crunchy raw veg with citrus and spice. The fennel seeds accentuate the fennel bulb's natural flavour, while the caraway is a good match for the brassica flavour of the kohlrabi. If you don't have all the spices just use those which you do. Cut the veg as thinly as you can (or use a mandolin).

SERVES 2-4 AS A STARTER OR SIDE DISH

1 courgette
1 fennel bulb, trimmed
   and fronds reserved
1 kohlrabi, peeled
several large mustard leaves,
   or other peppery salad
   leaves, e.g. rocket

For the vinaigrette
¾ tsp fennel seeds
¼ tsp caraway seeds
juice of ½ lemon
juice of ½ orange
5 tbsp extra virgin olive oil
salt and black pepper

Halve the courgette lengthways and slice each half crossways on the diagonal as thinly as you can. Quarter and core the fennel, then slice as thinly as you can. Cut the kohlrabi into matchsticks. Lay the mustard leaves on top of each other, roll up like a cigar and cut into thin ribbons.

Make the vinaigrette by grinding the seeds with a pestle and mortar and then mixing in the citrus juices and enough olive oil to balance their acidity. Season with salt and pepper to taste.

Toss all ingredients together, check for seasoning and serve garnished with the reserved fennel fronds.

fennel and chard gratin

vegetarian (if you use
a vegetarian alternative
to Parmesan)

SERVES 2

1 tbsp olive oil
knob of butter
1 large fennel bulb, core
    removed, thinly sliced
200g chard, leaves and
    stalks separated and
    stalks finely sliced
1 large garlic clove,
    crushed or finely chopped
splash of dry white wine
freshly grated nutmeg
3 tbsp double cream
4 tbsp breadcrumbs
    (optional)
2 tbsp grated Parmesan
    (or vegetarian alternative)
1 tsp finely grated lemon zest
salt and black pepper

Gratins are a great way of serving fennel if you prefer its softer, sweeter cooked flavour. They're a real Riverford staple. Adding greens gives the dish colour and extra nutrients.

Heat the oven to 190°C/Gas 5.

Heat the oil and butter in a pan. Add the fennel slices and chard stalks and cook very slowly, stirring now and then to stop it catching, until the fennel is lightly browned, about 15 minutes.

Meanwhile, boil the chard leaves in a pan of salted boiling water for 4 minutes. Drain, refresh in a bowl of cold water, then drain again. Use your hands to squeeze out any excess liquid then roughly chop.

Add the garlic to the fennel and cook for a further 2 minutes. Then add the wine, chard leaves and a few gratings of nutmeg and bubble for 2 minutes or so to reduce the wine. Stir in the cream, season with salt and pepper and transfer to a gratin dish.

In a bowl, mix together the breadcrumbs, if using, grated Parmesan and lemon zest and sprinkle over the fennel mixture. Bake for approximately 20 minutes, until the topping is golden.

VARIATION
Fry the fennel on its own or with a sliced onion, then toss with blanched spinach leaves instead of chard (you'll need a little more spinach – 300g should do it).

baked chicken with fennel and potatoes

easy

Oven bakes make for easy meals which can easily be scaled up or bulked out to feed more people. This one is good with a side dish of wilted spinach, spring or summer greens.

SERVES 2

1 large fennel bulb, cut into
    6 wedges, with the core
    intact to hold it together
    (see page 100)
400g new potatoes, scrubbed
    and cut into halves,
    or quarters if large
2 chicken legs
14 black olives, pitted
juice of ½ lemon
1 tbsp olive oil
2 garlic cloves, crushed
salt and black pepper

Heat the oven to 190°C/Gas 5.

Cook the fennel in a large pan of boiling water for a couple of minutes. Add the potatoes to the same pan and cook for a further 6 minutes. Drain.

Put the fennel and potatoes in a baking dish with the chicken and olives.

In a small bowl, whisk together the lemon juice, olive oil and garlic. Pour over the chicken and veg. Season with salt and pepper. Bake for about 45 minutes, until the chicken is cooked through. If the chicken needs a little longer, cover the dish loosely with foil to prevent the veg burning.

VARIATIONS
* If you haven't got new potatoes, use a waxy or all-rounder, such as Maris Piper, just not a stored, floury one.
* Use thick-cut, bone-in pork chops: fry them for a few minutes, to colour them, then add the chops to the veg after 30–35 minutes to finish cooking them in the oven.

roasted fennel and shallots
with lemon and olives

quick & easy

vegan

This is a great side dish for any kind of baked or grilled fish but to make it into a main course, add some chicken legs or thighs to the fennel before cooking or simply bulk it out with some plain boiled rice or quinoa. Save any feathery fennel fronds from your fennel bulbs to garnish.

SERVES 4

2 large or 3 small fennel
   bulbs, trimmed (fronds
   reserved) and each
   cut into 6 wedges
8 shallots, peeled and
   cut in half if large
12 pitted olives
   (green or black)
2 lemons, 1 juiced,
   1 cut into thick slices
oil for roasting
salt and black pepper

Heat the oven to 190°C/Gas 5.

Boil the fennel wedges in salted water for 5 minutes.

Transfer to a roasting tin with the shallots, olives and sliced lemon. Toss in just enough oil to coat. Season with salt and pepper and squeeze over the juice from the other lemon. Roast for approximately 45 minutes. The veg should be slightly caramelised.

Sprinkle with fennel fronds to serve.

VARIATIONS
* Try wedges of red or white onion in place of the shallots.
* Add a splash of dry white wine if you have any open.

may to september
green
beans

A few years ago, while staying with Darina Allen (doyenne of Ballymaloe Cookery School) at her cottage in West Cork in September, I ate more runner beans from her garden than I would have thought possible. They were so good I consumed bowls and bowls of them and almost gave up eating anything else. It was partly a mission to eat them before they went to waste and partly because they were so much better than the ones I had grown myself.

Runner beans are a gardener's bean. With their lush foliage and scarlet flowers, they are an impressive and rewarding crop that thrives in the protection of a garden. A really fresh runner bean, picked at its best, takes a lot of beating and as a commercial grower I have all but given up. Beans hate the wind and seem much happier in small, protected gardens and allotments than an open field and are at their best the day they are picked. We do better with dwarf French beans, which, with the help of crop covers, can be ready in late June, well ahead of the first runners in August.

To squeak or not to squeak? I like my beans minimally cooked with just a bit of squeak left in them; others like them firm but with no squeak. Don't think that you can make an old bean tender by cooking it for longer; if anything this just brings out the fibre. Be wary of runner beans after late September; with the end of the season's lower temperatures they may stay green and look okay but too often leave you picking bits from your teeth.

Guy

storage

Riverford sells three types of green bean: runner, French and flat. They're best stored in their bag in the vegetable drawer of the fridge where they should last up to a week before losing their snap.

prep

Most beans need topping and often tailing, which you can do with your fingers, or by lining them up in a neat row and using a knife. Runner beans benefit from de-stringing too: run a veg peeler down each side.

Many recipes call for French beans to be cooked whole, which helps retain their flavour (chopped vegetables give up more of their goodness to the water when boiled). If you need to slice your beans, it looks prettier to do it on an angle. Runner beans can be quite tough and are best sliced thinly. Flat beans can either be finely sliced or chopped into pieces.

eating green beans raw

Beans generally taste better cooked, if only briefly. However, finely sliced raw French beans work well in a crunchy salad, and whole ones can join a crudité selection for dunking into aioli, bagna cauda or another dip.

cooking

Most often we boil our beans briefly and then dress them up with a few flavourings for a hot side dish or substantial salad – but they can also be quickly fried, or slow-cooked.

boil/steam

Bring a large pot of salted water to a rolling boil and add the beans. Don't cover, as this dulls their bright green colour. Alternatively, put the beans in a steamer (in which case you will need to cover them). Whether green beans are better al dente or fully cooked is a matter of taste – cook them for between 4 and 8 minutes.

Drain and serve immediately, or, if you're using them in a salad or intending to reheat them later, plunge them into a bowl of ice-cold water, wait a few minutes then drain. This stops the cooking process so that they retain their bright green colour.

For a warm side dish we like them:

* Simply tossed with butter or oil, black pepper and flaky or coarse sea salt.

* Reheated in browned butter with some lightly fried sliced shallots, lemon juice and toasted almond flakes.

* Smothered in a rich tomato sauce, perhaps pepped up with black olives or chilli or topped with fried breadcrumbs.

* Tossed with one of the dressings on page 118–119.

GREEN BEAN SALAD IDEAS

Boiled green beans, especially French beans, make great salads. Drain and refresh them by dunking them in cold water then dress them while they're still slightly warm so they soak up the flavours. Try one of the recipes on page 118–119, or with:

* Crispy bacon, softened shallots and a wholegrain mustard and cider vinegar dressing made using the residual fat in the bacon pan.

* A vinaigrette made with tarragon vinegar, plenty of Dijon mustard and chopped capers, served topped with quartered hard-boiled eggs.

* Sun-dried tomatoes, or oven-roasted cherry tomatoes, black olives, a little crushed garlic and plenty of torn basil.

* Finely chopped or crushed garlic, toasted sesame seeds, sliced spring onions and a dressing made with soy sauce, rice wine vinegar, sesame oil and vegetable oil.

* Finely sliced red chilli and shallots, crushed roasted peanuts and a dressing of lime juice, rice wine vinegar, crushed garlic, brown sugar, fish sauce and vegetable oil.

green beans

stir-fry

You can fry whole French beans quickly in a little oil over high heat. Move them about the frying pan frequently and watch as they turn bright, almost luminous, green. An unusual but highly successful combination is garlic and honey: as the beans fry, throw in some roughly chopped garlic and a small spoonful of honey.

Alternatively, finely slice runner or flat beans into matchsticks and add to your stir-fry along with other quick-cooking veg.

braise

This method suits runner beans and flat beans and is common around the Eastern Mediterranean. Cut the beans on an angle into 5cm pieces and cook slowly in a covered heavy-bottomed saucepan with olive oil, finely chopped onions, garlic and tomatoes, stirring occasionally. The vegetables braise in their own juices so there's no need to add water. The longer and slower you cook them, the better they'll taste, so allow a good hour.

For a Southern US version, first fry streaky bacon, then sliced onions in the rendered fat, followed by a squeeze of tomato purée or dollop of passata. After a couple more minutes, add whole green beans, salt, pepper, a touch of cayenne and not quite enough water or stock to cover. Simmer gently on the stove, in a really low oven (120°C/Gas ½) or in a slow cooker for at least a couple of hours. Serve with bread to mop up the juices.

slow-roast

Like braised beans, slow-roast beans lose their bright green colour but develop a wonderfully rich flavour. Toss beans with olive oil, salt, pepper and sliced garlic until well coated. Spread over a roasting tin and roast at 190°C/Gas 5 until soft and caramelised, 30 minutes to 1 hour, depending on how dark you like them. You will need to check on the beans a few times: move them around the tin and turn them over so they caramelise evenly.

work well with...

* Alliums – garlic, onion, shallot
* Acid – lemon juice and vinegars
* Asian flavours – chilli, ginger, sesame, soy
* Cured pork – bacon, ham, prosciutto
* Herbs – basil, tarragon
* Honey and sugar
* Nuts – almonds, peanuts, walnuts
* Salty things – anchovies, capers, feta, olives, Parmesan
* Tomatoes
* Tuna

dressings for green beans

We've noted a weight of French beans in the recipes, but any green bean can be used; try sliced runners or flat green beans, broad beans or sugar snap peas if you like.

quick & easy

vegetarian

ingen no goma-ae

A Japanese dressing with sesame seeds – black ones make for dramatic contrast if you can find them. Serve as a side dish with simple grilled fish, or use as the main component of a stir-fry.

SERVES 4

3 tbsp sesame seeds
1 tbsp soft light brown sugar
1 good tsp brown rice miso paste
1 tbsp soy sauce
1 tbsp mirin (Japanese rice wine),
    or use a dry sherry
300g French beans, topped and tailed

Put the sesame seeds in a dry frying pan. Heat gently, stirring now and then, until they turn a toasty brown colour (be careful not to burn them; they turn very quickly).

Transfer half the seeds to a mortar, grind then add the sugar, miso paste, soy sauce and mirin and mix together so you have a thick dressing.

Boil the beans in a pan of salted water for 4–5 minutes, until tender but with a squeak when you bite into them. Drain, then toss the beans in the dressing and sprinkle over the remaining sesame seeds to serve.

roasted garlic dressing

This is good with grilled lamb, stirred into pasta or mixed with a tin of white beans, with some shredded mozzarella.

SERVES 4

1 head of garlic
olive oil
squeeze of lemon juice
300g French beans, topped and tailed
small handful of summer savory, marjoram
    or oregano leaves (or a mixture), chopped
    salt and black pepper

Heat the oven to 200°C/Gas 6.

Rub off any excess papery skin from the garlic head without separating the cloves. Slice the tip off, exposing the ends of the cloves. Place the garlic on a piece of foil, drizzle with a little olive oil and fold the foil round to seal it. Put it into a baking dish and bake until very soft, about 40 minutes to 1 hour, depending on size.

Remove the garlic from the oven, leave to cool slightly, then squeeze the soft pulp from the garlic cloves into a bowl. Use a fork to whisk them with about 4 tablespoons of olive oil (just enough to make it a thick dressing consistency) and season with salt and pepper. Add a squeeze of lemon juice to taste.

Boil the beans in salted water for 4–5 minutes, until tender when you bite into them. Draind, then transfer them to a bowl, add the herbs and pour over the dressing. Toss to combine then serve.

tahini dressing

Tasty with beans but equally good drizzled over lightly cooked summer carrots or greens. It makes enough for a side serving for about 4 people - leftover dressing will keep in the fridge for a couple of days, just give it a little whisk before using.

SERVES 4

2 tbsp light tahini
2 tbsp plain yoghurt
1 garlic clove, crushed or finely grated
2 tbsp extra virgin olive oil
juice of ½ lemon, more to taste
300g French beans, topped and tailed

In a bowl, stir the tahini with the yoghurt until you have a smooth paste. Whisk in the garlic, olive oil and lemon juice and add enough water to give the dressing the consistency of pouring cream.

Boil the beans in salted water for 4–5 minutes, until tender but with a squeak when you bite into them. Drain, then serve with the sauce drizzled over.

green beans with pancetta and sage

quick & easy

SERVES 4-6

500g French beans,
   topped and tailed
sunflower or light olive oil,
   for frying
250g pancetta, or bacon,
   cut into small cubes
8–10 sage leaves (depending
   on size), finely shredded
splash of balsamic or
   sherry vinegar
extra virgin olive oil
salt and pepper

*Serve as a side dish to chicken or toss through pasta to make it a
main meal in its own right, sprinkled with a little grated Parmesan.
Add a pinch of chilli flakes if you like heat. You could also use
a little very finely chopped rosemary instead of sage.*

Boil the beans in a pan of salted water for 3 minutes. Drain,
refresh in a bowl of ice cold water, then drain again once cooled.

In a pan, heat 1 tablespoon of oil over a medium heat. Add the
pancetta and fry on a high heat, turning now and then, for
approximately 5 minutes, until crispy. Turn the heat a little lower
and cook for a further 5 minutes to render any fat in the pancetta.

Add the beans and sage and stir for 2–3 minutes, to finish cooking
the beans.

Add a splash of vinegar, a little good olive oil and season with salt
and pepper to taste. Serve drizzled with any juices from the pan.

vegetarian 'Niçoise'

quick & easy

vegetarian

This is a vegetarian version of the Mediterranean summer classic. It uses capers in place of anchovies for saltiness - although you could use both. Marjoram is a similar herb to oregano, but slightly sweeter and with a floral aroma.

SERVES 4

600g new potatoes, scrubbed
  and cut into halves or
  quarters depending on size
8 eggs
300g French beans,
  topped and tailed
250g cherry tomatoes,
  cut in half crossways
2 large spring onions,
  very finely sliced
150g mixed salad leaves
about 20 pitted black olives
2 tbsp capers (if they are
  in brine, drain then
  soak in cold water for
  20 minutes then drain)
small handful of basil,
  shredded

For the dressing
4 tbsp olive oil
1 garlic clove, finely
  chopped or crushed
2 tsp Dijon mustard
½ lemon
3 or 4 fresh marjoram leaves
  or oregano sprigs,
  finely chopped
salt and black pepper

Put the potatoes in one pan with a good pinch of salt. Put the eggs in another pan. Cover both with water and put on a medium heat.

Once the eggs come to the boil, cook for 8 minutes, drain and put in a bowl of cold water. Once the potatoes come to the boil, cook for 10–12 minutes, until easily pierced with a sharp knife. Scoop the potatoes out of the water with a slotted spoon.

Add the beans to the potato water. Boil for 5 minutes, until they're tender but still have a squeak when you bite into them. Drain and refresh in cold water, then drain again.

To make the dressing, whisk the olive oil, garlic, mustard and a squeeze of lemon juice together in a large salad bowl. Stir in the chopped marjoram or oregano, then season with salt, pepper and extra lemon juice or oil to taste.

Add the potatoes, beans, tomatoes, spring onion, salad leaves, olives and capers to the bowl and toss together in the dressing.

Peel the hardboiled eggs – doing this in water is easiest – then cut them lengthways into quarters. Using a wet knife will help keep the yolk and white together. Tuck the eggs into the salad, scatter over the basil leaves and serve.

VARIATIONS
* Use roasted tomatoes for extra sweetness (pictured), see page 226.
* Add a few anchovies if you're not vegetarian.

bean and herb pasta

quick & easy

vegetarian (if you use
vegetarian Parmesan)

This is a really fresh, summery dish, with crunch from the
beans and tanginess from the lemon and Parmesan. You can
use any green bean (runner, French, finely sliced flat beans,
double-podded broad beans, even sugar snap peas).

SERVES 4

400g long pasta
   (e.g. spaghetti, linguine,
   tagliatelle – or whatever
   you have)
400g green beans, prepared,
   blanched until just tender,
   then refreshed in cold
   water – see pages 114–115;
   if using sugar snaps,
   just throw them in raw
4 tbsp extra virgin olive oil
2 garlic cloves, finely
   chopped, grated or
   crushed
zest and juice of 1 lemon,
   to taste
2 handfuls of mixed herbs
   (e.g. parsley, mint,
   chervil, tarragon,
   chives, dill), chopped
100g Parmesan or vegetarian
   alternative, grated
salt and pepper

Add the pasta to a large pan of salted boiling water and cook
according to the packet instructions. When you drain it, reserve
a couple of ladlefuls of the cooking water.

Meanwhile, heat the oil in a large frying pan. Add the beans,
garlic, lemon zest and juice and gently warm for 1 minute (keep
an eye on the garlic so it doesn't burn). Remove from the heat.

Add the pasta to the frying pan, along with the three quarters
of the fresh herbs and half the grated Parmesan. Season with
salt and pepper and toss gently to combine everything. Add
some of the reserved pasta water to loosen it up.

Transfer the pasta to a large serving bowl and sprinkle over
the remaining herbs and Parmesan to serve.

VARIATIONS
* Add some cooked and chopped spinach or chard leaves.
* Throw in some leftover roast chicken or fried bacon lardons.
* Swap the Parmesan for some crumbled blue cheese.
* Instead of using beans, grate two or three large courgettes
and fry them for a couple of minutes with the garlic and
lemon before tossing with the pasta.

kohlrabi
and may to july
summer
turnips

Kohlrabi and summer turnips are both fast-growing brassicas. In the field they have an extraordinary vigour and speed of growth that makes them one of the earliest new season vegetables, with the first UK crops ready for harvest in late May or early June. In the kitchen they both have a succulent tenderness and peppery sweetness that allows them to be grated, sliced or cut into matchsticks and eaten raw in salads, a bit like a radish. They are also delicious pickled or fermented as the Japanese or Koreans would treat a daikon or mouli. Turnips, with their firmer flesh and stronger flavour, are also happy roasted or used in stews.

Summer turnips are typically white- or purple-skinned with white flesh and measure 5–8cm across. They are not to be confused with winter turnips (typically brown or green with yellow flesh), which have no merit unless you're a hungry cow or sheep.

Kohlrabi vary in size but are generally about the size of a tennis ball. Pale greenish-white in colour, or sometimes tinged with purple, they feel hard to the touch and often come with pale green leaves attached on long stalks. Kirsty, one of our Riverford Cooks, compares them to an upside-down version of Mike, from the Disney film, *Monsters, Inc.*, (she hopes this encourages kids to try them).

Guy

storage

Kohlrabi and summer turnips will stay firm in the fridge for a week or even two. As with carrots and beetroot, any leaves are better removed or they will suck moisture from the veg. The leaves are edible and can be stir-fried or added to stews (see page 129).

prep

Only the youngest, smallest specimens have tender skins, so after washing kohlrabi and turnips you will probably need to peel them. First trim away any stems. (If the kohlrabi's irregular skin is too much for your peeler, switch to a paring knife.)

Separate any leaves from their stalks and wash in a bowl of water. If not cooking them immediately, spin dry and store in a plastic box or bag in the fridge.

For boiling, braising and roasting, cut them into chunky wedges or batons. If you are planning to eat them raw, kohlrabi and turnips are best grated or cut into very thin slices or fine matchsticks.

eating kohlrabi and summer turnips raw

Kohlrabi and summer turnips are good – some would say best – raw; they are fresh, crunchy and peppery, rather like radishes. They make fantastic Asian coleslaws, solo or paired with carrots, celeriac and cabbage.

cooking

Cut into matchsticks, turnips and kohlrabi can be added to stir-fries (see page 137). Cut into slices and layered with starchy potatoes, they make a tasty gratin (see page 137). Like most vegetables, they can be boiled into soup, or added to a meat stew about 30–40 minutes before the end of its cooking time. Or for an easy side dish, cut kohlrabi and turnips into chunks, toss with oil and seasoning and roast in the oven at 210°C/Gas 7 for 30 minutes.

braise

Cut the vegetables into chunky pieces. Heat a good knob of butter in a wide pan, add a single layer of the veg and season with salt and a good sprinkling of sugar or drizzle of honey. Add a bay leaf or thyme sprig if you have them, plus a dash of dry white wine or vermouth if you're feeling flash. Pour in water to half cover the vegetables and bring to a boil. Reduce to a simmer, cover and cook gently, stirring occasionally, until the vegetables are just tender, about 20 minutes. Add more water if the pan starts to run dry before the vegetables are cooked.

As the vegetables become tender, remove the lid and let the excess water boil away. Now cook them a few minutes longer, tossing in the sweet buttery glaze left in the pan. If you like, keep frying until they caramelise; this works a treat with young turnips. Check the seasoning, add a dash of vinegar to brighten the flavour and finish with chopped herbs.

work well with...

* Acid – citrus, vinegars
* Alliums – garlic, onions, shallots
* Apple
* Carrot
* Chilli
* Dairy – butter, cream, yoghurt, Parmesan
* Herbs – chives, chervil, coriander, dill, parsley
* Mustard and mustard seeds
* Sesame
* Sweet things – dried fruits, honey, sugar

USING KOHLRABI LEAVES AND TURNIP GREENS

* Treat kohlrabi leaves like spring greens. Strip them from their tough stems and rinse. Boil in salted water until tender – a couple of minutes, then drain and refresh. Warm in a little oil or butter to serve.

* Turnip greens are more tender. Treat them like spinach: wash well and wilt in a hot pan with oil or butter and seasoning. Alternatively, add them to a stew or soup shortly before the end of cooking. Or blanch them briefly then whizz into a green purée and use to garnish a turnip soup.

turnips caramelised with butter and wine

quick & easy

vegetarian

SERVES 6 AS A SIDE DISH

700g small or medium-
    sized turnips
50g unsalted butter
200ml white wine,
    preferably sweet
1 tbsp caster sugar
salt and black pepper

Riverford Cook Anna learnt this indulgent method for cooking turnips while working at Chez Panisse, the restaurant in California which inspired Guy to open the Riverford Field Kitchen. There they use dessert wine in the recipe for extra floral sweetness. The recipe works best with baby turnips cut into quarters, although medium-sized ones also work well (avoid big, tired-looking ones). Caramelised turnips are a great match for roast lamb and duck.

Unless they are baby, peel the turnips. Cut lengthways into quarters if small, or sixths or eighths if bigger. You should have even-sized wedges.

Place the wedges in a frying pan that is not quite wide enough to hold them in one layer. They should look a little crowded, but not be piled more than two deep.

Add the butter, wine, sugar and a generous pinch of salt then pour in cold water to almost cover. Cook over moderate heat, moving the turnips around occasionally, for about 15 minutes or until tender. By the time the turnips are tender, the water should have completely evaporated, leaving just the sugary butter in the pan. If the water is evaporating too fast, add a little more.

Once the water has evaporated and the turnips are tender, continue cooking them, shaking the pan occasionally, until the wedges are nicely caramelised around their edges. Check the seasoning and serve hot.

pickled kohlrabi

quick & easy

vegan

SERVES 4

1 large kohlrabi
250ml white or
    red wine vinegar
1 tbsp sea salt
1 tbsp honey
1 garlic clove, thinly sliced
1 tsp peppercorns
1 fresh chilli or ½ dried
    chilli, flaked
1 tbsp fresh ginger, grated
2 bay leaves
1 tsp black peppercorns

Kohlrabi has a unique crisp, fresh taste when raw (see page 128) but can get lost in a crowd of other flavours when it tends to offer more texture than taste. Turning kohlrabi into a pickle with a few aromatics lends it a sharper edge and is a good way to use up the whole piece in one go. It also extends the shelf life. At its most basic the pickling liquid can be made with just the water, vinegar, honey and salt – so vary the herbs and spices as you like.

Peel the kohlrabi, slice thinly and cut the slices into fine matchstick-thin shreds (or use a mandolin).

Put the vinegar, salt and honey in a pan with 250ml water and bring to the boil.

Mix the kohlrabi with the remaining ingredients in a bowl and then pack into a sterilised preserving jar. Tip the hot liquid over them, making sure it reaches the top of the jar and covers everything. Close the lid and allow to cool.

Keep in the fridge and use within a couple of weeks. It is best left for at least 3 days before eating.

IDEAS FOR USING PICKLED KOHLRABI
* Fold into coleslaw and salads for a burst of sharpness.
* Add to burgers, wraps and sandwiches.
* Use as a side with warm dishes like bangers and mash or grilled pork chops for the same contrast you would get from sauerkraut.
* Throw into stir-fries or noodle dishes at the last minute.

potato and kohlrabi gratin with lemon thyme

long slow cook

vegetarian (if you use
a vegetarian cheese)

A mandolin really helps to get the potato and kohlrabi slices as thin as possible and will speed up the cooking time. Lemon thyme is quite unusual; use ordinary thyme if you can't find any but lemon thyme has a delicate flavour that's especially suited to summer dishes. It's a good one to plant, or keep a small pot of it. Serve this as a side dish - it's particularly good with pork, or as a vegetarian main course with steamed summer greens.

**SERVES 4 AS A SIDE,
2-3 AS A MAIN**

small knob of butter
   for greasing
200ml double cream (or see
   Variation below)
100ml milk
2 large or 3 smaller lemon
   thyme sprigs, leaves only
2 garlic cloves, crushed or
   finely grated
500g potatoes, very finely
   sliced
1 large kohlrabi (about 500g),
   peeled and very finely
   sliced
3 tbsp finely grated
   Parmesan or vegetarian
   alternative
salt and pepper

Heat the oven to 180°C/Gas 4. Grease a small (approx. 25 x 15cm) gratin or baking dish with a little butter.

Put the cream, milk, lemon thyme and garlic into a small saucepan. Heat until steaming, then remove from the heat and leave to infuse for 10 minutes.

Arrange alternate layers of potato and kohlrabi in the gratin dish, seasoning each layer. Pour over the infused cream and cover the dish with foil. Bake for 1–1½ hours (depending on how thinly you've sliced the potatoes and kohlrabi), until the veg is just tender and easily pierced with the tip of a sharp knife. Remove the foil and scatter over the Parmesan. Return to the oven for 15–20 minutes, until the cheese is golden and the gratin bubbling.

VARIATIONS
* Substitute the cream for equal parts of vegetable stock and milk.
* Use turnips instead of the kohlrabi.

lamb stew with baby summer turnips

long slow cook

freezable

Lamb stew needn't be a dark and heavy affair. Summer turnips have a sweet, almost radish-like taste, that's lighter than their winter cousins. White wine instead of red and the addition of some vibrant green veg and herbs at the end also lighten things.

SERVES 4

olive oil
1 onion, finely diced
1 carrot, finely diced
2 celery sticks, finely diced
2 garlic cloves,
    finely chopped
1kg lamb neck, cut into
    3–4cm chunks
1 glass of dry white wine
1 bay leaf
500ml hot chicken stock
4 baby turnips, peeled
100g French beans, topped,
    tailed and thinly sliced
100g double-podded broad
    beans (see page 61)
2 tsp Dijon mustard
    (optional)
1 mint sprig, leaves
    only, chopped
small bunch of
    parsley, chopped
½ lemon
salt and pepper

Heat the oven to 170°C/Gas 3½.

Heat a little olive oil in a large casserole pot and gently cook the onion, carrot, celery and garlic over a low heat until beginning to soften and take a little colour, about 15 minutes. Remove from the pan and set to one side.

Season the lamb with salt and pepper. Turn the heat up to medium, add some more oil to the pan and brown the lamb on all sides. When nicely golden, add the wine and scrape the base of the pan with a wooden spoon to deglaze. Cook until the wine is reduced by half.

Return the veg to the pan, add the bay leaf and pour in the stock so that the lamb is just covered. Season with salt and pepper, cover the casserole and transfer to the oven for 30 minutes.

Cut the turnips into thick wedges, add to the casserole and cook for a further hour, or until the lamb is tender.

Add the French and broad beans to the pot and simmer on the stove for about 5 minutes to cook them. Just before serving, stir in the mustard, parsley and mint leaves and a squeeze of lemon juice.

VARIATIONS
* Use a jointed chicken or duck legs or diced shoulder of lamb instead of the neck. Shoulder will take longer to cook, 30 minutes or so extra, so add the beans and turnips later – after 1 hour.
* Or omit the meat: brown the turnips in place of the lamb and use vegetable stock; add a handful of pearl barley, spelt or bulghur wheat and simmer until the turnips are tender, about 30 minutes.

kohlrabi and peanut stir-fry

quick & easy

vegetarian

Kohlrabi takes on spicy flavourings well, so is a good veg to use in Asian cooking, either in curries, stir-fries or even simply braised (see page 129) with aromatic Szechuan pepper and star anise in the braising liquid.

SERVES 3-4

250g egg noodles

2 tbsp sesame oil

2 tbsp sunflower oil

1 large or 2 small carrots, peeled and cut into thin matchsticks

1 large kohlrabi, peeled, cut into thin slices, then into matchsticks

2 garlic cloves, crushed or finely grated

3–4cm piece of fresh ginger, peeled and finely grated

1 red chilli, deseeded and finely chopped (leave the seeds in for more heat; optional)

1 bunch of spring onions, finely sliced on the diagonal

150g sugar snap peas, or use chopped green beans, or a mix of both

3 tbsp hoisin sauce

2 tbsp soy sauce

1 generous tbsp crunchy peanut butter

3 tbsp unsalted peanuts, toasted and chopped

squeeze of lime juice, to taste

handful of coriander leaves, roughly chopped (optional)

Cook the noodles according to the packet instructions, then toss with the sesame oil to prevent them from sticking together.

Heat the sunflower oil in a wok, add the carrot, kohlrabi, garlic, ginger and chilli, if using, and stir-fry on a high heat for 3 minutes.

Add the noodles with the spring onions and the sugar snap peas or green beans and cook for a further 2 minutes.

Stir in the hoisin sauce, soy sauce, peanut butter, chopped peanuts and 2 tablespoons of water (add a little more water for more of a sauce) and heat through.

Serve with a little lime juice squeezed over and sprinkled with the chopped coriander, if using.

VARIATIONS

* Add some sliced pork fillet or beef strips to this if you're not vegetarian, or throw in some leftover roast meat.
* Try cashews instead of peanuts.
* Add some sliced mushrooms – shiitake would be good.

may to june
new
potatoes

New potatoes were traditionally grown on the coastal fringes of western Britain, including the Channel Islands and the Isles of Scilly where maritime air warmed by the Gulf Stream gave protection from frost and allowed planting in January for lifting in May when prices were at their peak. These fields were fertilised by seaweed gathered on local beaches, which may have contributed to the flavour.

Good things come to those who wait but growers and traders have become impatient. Sadly, quick growth, pushed on by water and nitrogen fertiliser and aided by breeding for precocity alone has produced some early potatoes which are staggeringly tasteless. Perhaps my taste buds are fading but even Jersey Royals with their with their **EU PDO** (Protected Designation of Origin) status, seem pretty average to me today.

We are more patient and seldom start harvesting before June with slow-growing varieties like Colleen and hope to move to our favourite variety, the reliably delicious Charlotte, by the end of the month. Through June and much of July the tubers are loose-skinned and very delicate as a result. Without the protection of a set skin they should be kept in the fridge and used within a week. Wash loose-skinned potatoes under the tap and rub off the worst of the skin before cooking. By July set skins are established and your potatoes should keep better.

Guy

new potatoes

varieties

We grow a few different varieties of new potato. They are all good simply boiled or cooked according to the various other suggestions opposite. Through the late spring/early summer, you're likely to see:

CHARLOTTE A classic new potato with a light yellow flesh. Well known and loved.

COLLEEN High yielding and uniform (as much as an organic potato can be!).

MARIS PEER Has a lovely fresh flavour.

LADY CHRISTL Ideal for growing in a container, if you fancy trying your hand at a bit of patio gardening.

OSTARA Not so well known, but a creamy-fleshed, all-round new potato

storage

Like all potatoes, new potatoes like to be kept dirty and in the dark. Leave them in their paper bag and store somewhere cool. Loose-skinned potatoes should be kept in the fridge and used within a week; set skins will last a little longer, a couple of weeks or more.

prep

New potatoes' loose, young skins provide much of the potato's flavour, and nutrition. Don't peel them, just give them a gentle scrub in cold water; their flaky little skins may look tatty, but better taste over appearance. Most of our recipes require keeping the potatoes whole, only halving or quartering them if they're particularly big.

cooking

New potatoes are at their best boiled and eaten with a little butter and some flaky or coarse sea salt. As the season progresses, though, we often turn to the frying pan and oven for a bit of variation. The following methods apply to all new and salad potatoes.

boil

Without salt, potatoes are bland, so when boiling potatoes use plenty; the water should taste as salty as the sea.

Place the potatoes in a saucepan and cover with cold water by a few centimetres. Add lots of salt and bring to the boil. Reduce the heat and simmer until the potatoes are cooked through, about 15 minutes. Test with a paring knife – it should slice in easily right to the middle. Adding sprigs of fresh mint to the cooking water is very British, but you can experiment with other herbs, too: lovage works a treat. Drain and allow to steam-dry for a couple of minutes in the colander.

IDEAS FOR USING BOILED NEW POTATOES

* Keep it simple: butter, salt, pepper and some chopped mint, parsley, chives or lovage.

* Go garlicky: finely slice a bulb of wet garlic (see page 248) and gently fry it in a generous knob of butter until softened. Toss cooked potatoes in the garlicky butter and serve immediately.

* Celebrate summer's arrival: separately blanch broad beans (see page 61), asparagus (see page 34) and peas and gently mix with potatoes along with little strips of fried streaky bacon and its rendered fat.

* Go Genoese: cut the boiled potatoes into cubes or slices and toss gently with cooked pasta, blanched green beans (see page 115) and pesto. Add a little cream or crème fraîche to make it more saucy.

* Make a warm salad: try crumbled blue cheese, fried bacon and watercress, or lemon juice, lemon zest, Dijon mustard and sliced spring onions. Once they're dressed, let the hot potatoes sit for at least 10 minutes to absorb the flavours.

* Add raw new potatoes to a simmering stew around half an hour before it's done. They work well in lamb, fish and vegetable stews.

* Crush overcooked or leftover boiled potatoes: warm them in a pan on a low heat with some olive oil, then press them against the side of the pan with a spoon, being careful not to let them stick or burn. Add some butter and/or a dash of cream or crème fraîche and plenty of herbs.

* Make hash browns: grate some boiled spuds, season, press into discs (perhaps with a small amount of grated onion) and fry in oil or butter until crispy and brown on both sides. Serve as part of a fry-up or with a poached egg and some smoked salmon.

new potatoes

POTATO SALAD

Debates rage over the right way to make potato salad: a creamy dressing or vinaigrette? Should the potatoes be sliced, cubed or roughly smashed? Ultimately it's down to personal preference. For maximum flavour, boil the potatoes whole, even if you will later peel or slice them. Dress them while still warm, so they absorb the flavours, and let the salad sit for at least 10 minutes before serving. We've included a couple of our favourite recipes on page 145, but you could also experiment with:

* cream, crème fraîche, mayonnaise and/or yoghurt in the dressing.

* smooth, wholegrain or powdered mustard (made up with a little water).

* capers, cornichons, olives, piccalilli or another relish for punch.

* sliced boiled eggs, fried bacon, crumbled cheese, sun-dried tomatoes or flaked smoked fish.

* handfuls of herbs (parsley, chives, chervil, mint, lovage and dill are all good), watercress, rocket, peppery lettuce leaves or endive for greenery.

* chopped radishes, kohlrabi, cucumbers or celery for crunch.

stove

This is an ingenious way to cook small, round potatoes in their own moisture, which really intensifies their flavour. Fill a frying pan, preferably non-stick, with one layer of scrubbed potatoes. Drizzle over some oil or dot around some butter (or lard), season, and add just a splash of water. Cover tightly and cook over a low heat, shaking the pan occasionally, until the potatoes are tender to the middle and golden on the outside. Depending on the size of your potatoes and how tightly the lid fits the pan, this will take anything from 20 to 40 minutes. The potatoes will cook in their own juices and steam. Test them with a sharp knife from time to time.

roast/bake

Cut larger potatoes into halves or quarters so that all pieces are roughly the same size. Toss with olive oil, seasoning, smashed garlic cloves and robust herbs such as rosemary, sage or thyme. Spread them over a baking tray and roast in an oven set at 210°C/Gas 6, until cooked through. Alternatively, wrap them up in a parchment parcel, folding and stapling the edges to seal, place on a tray and bake. Either way, they'll take around 40 minutes. If the barbecue is going, you can wrap them in foil and bake over hot coals. Turn the foil packet over from time to time and start testing after 20 minutes.

For extra-crispy roast new potatoes, parboil them first in well-salted water. Drain when they are half-cooked, let steam-dry in the colander for a few minutes, then gently squish each one with your hand or the back of a wooden spoon. Arrange on a lightly oiled baking tray and drizzle with more oil and seasoning. Roast at 220°C/Gas 7 for 20–25 minutes until golden brown and crunchy. Check on them halfway through the cooking time; they may need turning over or moving around to roast evenly.

HELPING POTATOES KEEP THEIR SHAPE

If your potatoes tend to fall apart as they boil, try starting them off in salted cold water as usual, slightly acidifying the water with lemon juice or cream of tartar, then raise the temperature of the water to just short of a simmer. Hold them at this temperature until they're cooked through and they should retain their shape.

work well with...

* Acid – lemon, pickles, vinegar
* Alliums – garlic, onions, spring onions
* Bacon and pancetta
* Butter
* Cream, crème fraîche, soured cream, etc.
* Eggs
* Fish – oily, smoked, white
* Herbs, especially chives, dill, mint, parsley
* Saffron
* Salty things – anchovies, blue cheese, capers, olives

potato salad with spring onion and chimichurri

quick & easy

vegan

Chimichurri, a parsley and garlic sauce, is traditionally served with grilled meats in South America so this makes a perfect barbecue salad. For a more homely, English version, or if serving with lamb, use a few dabs of mint sauce in place of the chimichurri.

SERVES 4

4 garlic cloves, finely chopped
large bunch of flat-leaf parsley,
    finely chopped
2 tsp finely chopped oregano leaves
2 tbsp red wine vinegar
4 tbsp olive oil
1/2 tsp chilli flakes
1kg freshly boiled new potatoes
4 spring onions, finely sliced

Mash the garlic to a paste with the back of your knife. Mix it with the herbs and vinegar in a large bowl. Add the olive oil and chilli flakes. Season with salt and pepper and mix well. Stir in the potatoes and spring onions.

potato salad with chives and mustard

quick & easy

vegan

An oldie but a goldie. There are many possible variations: try replacing the olive oil with soured cream or crème fraîche, or adding diced and crisply fried bacon or pancetta.

SERVES 4

1 tbsp wholegrain mustard
1 tbsp Dijon mustard
1 tbsp cider vinegar
2 tbsp olive oil
small bunch of chives, finely snipped
1kg freshly boiled new potatoes
salt and pepper

Mix together the mustards and vinegar in a large bowl. Pour in the olive oil slowly, whisking all the time. Add the chives, season well with salt and pepper and fold in the spuds.

caramelised potatoes

quick & easy

SERVES 6-8

1.6kg new potatoes
7 tbsp mild flavoured,
    runny honey
3 tbsp caster sugar
150ml hot water
2 tbsp apple or cider vinegar
35g butter
a few thyme sprigs
salt and pepper

In Denmark this side dish is traditionally eaten with roast pork or duck, and sometimes with pork sausages. The potatoes are quite sweet so try to have some sour elements on the plate as well as plenty of salt on the table. This recipe comes courtesy of Mia Kristensen of CPH Good Food, who offers classes in Copenhagen to help home cooks translate the new Nordic diet movement into achievable, tasty and healthy home cooking.

Boil the potatoes in well-salted water until tender but still holding their shape well, 10–15 minutes depending on their size. Drain, cool and carefully peel the skins (or leave on as we do with our very new potatoes and they work beautifully). This step can be done a day ahead; store the potatoes in the fridge.

Melt the honey and sugar in a wide, heavy-bottomed, preferably non-stick frying pan over a medium heat until it starts to brown. Add the water and vinegar and stir. The sugar mass will harden, but just keep stirring until it starts to dissolve.

Stir in the butter, thyme and cooked potatoes. Leave to simmer until the water has gone and the potatoes are nicely coated with caramel. Season to taste and serve hot.

flavourings for roast new potatoes

The biggest mistake that people make when adding flavouring to roast potatoes is to throw all the ingredients into the roasting tin together, so that the more delicate ingredients burn by the time the dish is finished. The three recipes here should put a stop to that.

chorizo, roast peppers and almonds

quick & easy

SERVES 4

1kg new potatoes
100g chorizo, diced into 5mm cubes
2 roasted red peppers roughly sliced (see page 160)
2 tsp red wine or sherry vinegar.
50g flaked almonds, lightly toasted

Roast the potatoes following the instructions on page 143, but take the potatoes out of the oven after 25 minutes, just as they are starting to take on some colour. Add the chorizo, peppers and vinegar to the tray and mix well.

Return to the oven and roast for a further 15 minutes. Sprinkle over the almonds before serving.

VARIATION
For a meat-free version, replace the chorizo with 1/2 a tablespoon of paprika.

Bombay spice

quick & easy

vegan

SERVES 4

1kg new potatoes
4 tomatoes, roughly chopped
1 tsp ground turmeric
1 tsp garam masala
1 tsp cumin seeds, toasted and roughly crushed
1/2 tsp chilli flakes
1 red onion, finely sliced
handful of coriander, chopped
salt and pepper

Roast the potatoes following the instructions on page 143, but take the potatoes out of the oven after 25 minutes, just as they are starting to take on some colour, and add the tomatoes and all the spices. Mix well, return to the oven and roast for a further 15 minutes.

Before serving, scatter over the red onions and coriander and check the seasoning.

garlic, herbs and lemon

quick & easy

vegan

SERVES 4

6 garlic cloves
1 lemon, cut into 6 wedges
a few small thyme sprigs
a few small rosemary sprigs
1kg new potatoes
salt and pepper

Lightly crush the garlic cloves and the herbs with the back of a knife or in a pestle and mortar.

Roast the potatoes following the instructions on page 143, but take the potatoes out of the oven after 25 minutes, just as they are starting to take on some colour, and add the garlic, lemon and herbs. Mix well, return to the oven and roast for a further 15 minutes. Check the seasoning before serving.

new potatoes baked in a bag

quick & easy

vegan

SERVES 4 AS A SIDE

600g new potatoes
2 tbsp olive oil
1 bay leaf
salt and pepper

'In a bag', or 'en papillote' if you're feeling fancy, is a classic way of cooking all sorts of ingredients (see the fish and fennel recipe on page 105 and our other ideas for potatoes overleaf). With new potatoes you end up in a middle ground between roasted and steamed. We serve these all summer in the Field Kitchen, torn open at the table. To make the bag, take a large square of baking parchment and fold it in half. Fold three of the sides over firmly two or three times and secure with a couple of staples, leaving an opening at the top. You can comfortably cook up to about 600g of potatoes in one bag before it becomes too crowded and the heat distribution is affected, but there's no reason you can't make smaller bags to serve one to each person.

Heat the oven to 200°C/Gas 6. Cut the potatoes into pieces no bigger than 3–4cm (in half if small). While still wet, mix them in a bowl with the oil and a generous seasoning of salt and pepper.

Tip the potatoes into the bag with all the oil and water from the bowl. Pop in the bay leaf and any other flavourings (see overleaf). Fold the top of the bag over two or three times and secure with three staples, one in each corner and one in the middle.

Sit the parcel on a baking tray and bake in the oven for about 40 minutes. To test, push down on the corner of the bag – a potato should crush under a little pressure. To serve, flip into a large serving bowl and tear open the top of the bag. Keep track of the staples!

OTHER IDEAS FOR WHAT TO PUT IN YOUR PAPILLOTE OF POTATOES

* **BUTTER AND HERBS** Mix in 50g of diced butter and a few sprigs of thyme, rosemary, oregano and/or sage.

* **LEMON AND GARLIC** Peel 3 generous strips of peel from a lemon. Crush 3 unpeeled garlic cloves with the heel of your hand. Mix the peel and garlic with the potatoes.

* **WET GARLIC/SPRING ONIONS AND WINE** Trim and finely slice the wet garlic or spring onions and add to the potatoes along with about 80ml white wine or vermouth and 25g diced butter.

* **MUSHROOMS AND GARLIC** Finely slice 3 large Portobello mushrooms or 200g chestnut mushrooms. Fry quickly over a high heat in 1 tablespoon of oil or butter until starting to darken. Add to the potatoes with 2 lightly crushed garlic cloves and a thyme sprig. You could also add a few drops of truffle oil at the end if you're feeling posh.

* **FENNEL AND ORANGE** Trim and finely slice a bulb of fennel. Toast and coarsely crush a teaspoon of fennel seeds. Peel 2 large strips of peel from an orange. Mix the fennel, fennel seeds and orange peel strips into the potatoes, along with a shot of aniseed liquor e.g. Pernod or Pastis if you have any to hand. You could also add a handful of chopped tarragon leaves just before serving.

chicken, broad bean and new potato stew

easy

SERVES 4

3 tbsp sunflower or light olive
  oil, for frying
4 chicken thighs and
  4 drumsticks
2 small or 1 large onion,
  finely sliced
2 garlic cloves, finely
  chopped or grated
500ml dry cider
2 bay leaves
300ml good chicken or veg
  stock
200g podded broad beans
800g new potatoes, cut in
  half or quarters,
  depending on size
2 tbsp double cream or
  crème fraîche
2 tbsp wholegrain mustard,
  or to taste
large handful of tarragon
  leaves, roughly chopped
salt and pepper

We love one-pot dinners; this one is simple to cook and shouts of summer. If you like a thicker sauce, remove the chicken and veg once cooked, then boil the creamy sauce to reduce it down a little, before adding the mustard and tarragon to finish. Try this with other beans or peas and if you haven't got cider, use a glass of white wine and a little more stock, or just a good flavoured stock.

Heat the oil in a large pan, add the chicken and fry over a medium–high heat, turning now and then, until golden brown. (Don't overcrowd the pan – cook in batches if necessary.) Remove to a plate.

Add the onion to the same pan, with a little more oil if needed, and fry over a low heat for 10 minutes, stirring now and then and adding a splash of water if it looks like catching.

Add the garlic and fry, stirring, for 2 more minutes. Add the cider, bring to the boil and let it bubble away for 5 minutes.

Return the chicken to the pan, along with any juices from the plate. Add the bay leaves and stock and season with salt and pepper. Reduce the heat, cover and simmer for 20 minutes.

While the chicken pot is simmering, cook the broad beans for 2–3 minutes in another pan of boiling water. Drain, refresh in a bowl of cold water, then remove the outer skin. Leave to one side.

Add the potatoes to the chicken pot. Cover and simmer for a further 20 minutes, or until the potatoes are just tender. Check the chicken is cooked through (pierce the thickest part of the joint with a sharp knife; the juice should run clear) – simmer a little longer if needed. Keep an eye on the liquid and add a splash more stock or water if it looks like drying out.

Add the broad beans and cream and simmer for 5 minutes. Stir in the mustard to taste, then the tarragon. Check the seasoning before serving.

july to october
peppers

Peppers, along with tomatoes, aubergines, potatoes and most of their *Solanaceae* cousins are native to Central and South America. In 500 years their variant forms, along with chillies, have become indispensable in kitchens around the world but life would have been easier for UK growers if the conquistadors had left them to the Incas and the Aztecs. It is virtually impossible to grow a reliable crop in our climate, and even with the help of a tunnel or greenhouse the season is just a few short weeks in autumn. Heating the greenhouse and even using supplementary lighting will extend the season and increase yield but, according to our sums, a UK crop grown in this way has 10 times the carbon footprint of a pepper grown in Spain and trucked north, which is surely insanely environmentally destructive, even to the most bellicose localist. We make no apologies for importing the majority of our peppers from our growers in Andalusia, and during the summer from our French farm in the Vendée.

The cook, rather than the farmer in me, likes the versatility peppers offer, adding colour, texture and flavour as well as lots of vital nutrients, to summer dishes.

Guy

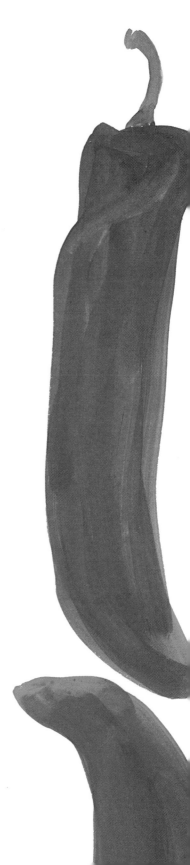

peppers

varieties

BELL The standard mild, sweet, fleshy pepper. Immature fruit are green and slightly bitter, becoming sweeter as they ripen and turn yellow, orange or red.

RAMIRO (AKA ROMANO) These long, tapering, irregularly shaped peppers are usually dark red, but occasionally we send out green ones in the veg boxes. Sweeter and more flavoursome than the bell pepper, they're largely interchangeable with them in recipes.

PADRÓN Small green Spanish peppers. The majority are mild and sweet, but about 10 per cent can be extremely hot and sadly there's no way of telling – you just have to take the risk (see also page 158).

SWEET MINI Miniature bell peppers in hues of yellow, orange and red, these can be used like other peppers. They come into their own when stuffed or roasted whole.

storage

Peppers keep well in the salad drawer of the fridge for a week or two. Even when a little wrinkled, they can still taste great.

prep

Some cooks peel their peppers before cooking to prevent little curls of skin floating to the top of the dish, but we rarely find the time!

Whether or not you peel them, you will need to remove the stems, seeds and ribs before proceeding. There are various ways to do this easily:

* For bell peppers: lop off the stem and stand the pepper upside down. Use a sharp knife to cut away the lobes of flesh, leaving behind a skeleton of ribs and seeds attached to the stem end at the bottom.

* With any pepper (this wastes less flesh): cut the pepper in half lengthways. Pull out the stem from each half with the core and seeds attached to it. Tear out any remaining pithy ribs and tap out loose seeds.

* If you want pepper boats to stuff: halve the peppers lengthways and use a small, sharp knife to cut out the pithy core and its seeds, leaving the stem end intact so that the filling won't run out.

* If you want whole peppers to stuff or cut into rings: use a small, sharp knife to cut out a circle around the stem end. Pull it out, taking with it the pithy core and seeds. Tap out loose seeds. You can tidy up the top to act as lid for stuffed peppers.

* Sometimes you'll find a baby pepper nestled inside; this is the cook's snack!

eating peppers raw

Finely sliced or diced, peppers make a colourful, crunchy addition to salads, but they are more flavoursome when cooked.

cooking

Peppers respond well to slow-frying and braising, becoming soft and intensely sweet. They can also be roasted in the oven to similar effect, or charred under the grill and peeled to reveal the luscious flesh. If time is short, slice them finely for a stir-fry.

slow-fry/braise

Fried slowly in oil, green peppers, onions and celery are the base for many Cajun soups and stews, including jambalaya and gumbo. Red peppers can be used in the same way and make a tasty base for Spanish-style dishes, along with onion, garlic and tomato. The trick is to fry them long and slow.

Slow-fried/braised peppers can also be a dish in their own right. The classic example is an Italian peperonata: put chopped red peppers and garlic into a heavy-bottomed saucepan with a glug of olive oil, season with salt and let the peppers cook in their juices over a low heat. You can speed up the process by putting the lid on to trap the steam, but they'll still take at least 30 minutes to become really soft. Finish with torn basil and a dash of balsamic vinegar. Peperonata tastes even better once cool, and keeps in the fridge for a few days.

USING SLOW-FRIED/ BRAISED PEPPERS

* On toast with a selection of antipasti – olives, pickles and salami.

* Eat as a side dish with pork or lamb chops, or pan-fried tuna steaks.

* Make a Hungarian-style stew: add paprika and caraway and/or fennel seeds to the peppers and fry for a few minutes. Brown cubes of pork shoulder in a little oil or butter then add to the peppers along with enough white wine and/or stock to barely cover. Partially cover with the lid and simmer gently for a couple of hours until the pork is tender. Serve with soured cream stirred through and boiled potatoes on the side.

* Make a Middle Eastern shakshuka: include onions and tomatoes when braising and add fresh or dried red chilli and a little ground cumin, coriander and black pepper. When the peppers are soft, make indentations and crack an egg into each one. Cover and simmer gently for 5–10 minutes until the eggs are set.

* As a sandwich filler, with sliced mozzarella and rocket leaves.

char and peel

This is another good way to bring out the best in peppers, giving them an even sweeter flavour, although it requires a little more time than roasting. There are several methods:

IN THE OVEN Rub whole peppers with a little oil and roast on a baking sheet at 200°C/Gas 6 until collapsed and blackened, a good 45 minutes or more. Use tongs or a fish slice to turn them over once or twice while cooking.

UNDER THE GRILL Halve the peppers lengthways and remove their stems, cores and seeds. Rub with a little oil and place skin-side up on a baking sheet. Position 8–10cm below a grill pre-heated to high and grill until the skin is blackened and the flesh has softened, about 20–30 minutes.

ON THE BARBECUE This gives a deliciously smoky flavour. Grill whole peppers over a medium–high heat, turning them every few minutes until blackened and soft, about 20 minutes.

Once charred, tip the peppers into a bowl and cover with a plate or cling film so that they cool in their own steam, or put them in a plastic bag. This loosens their skins. When they're cool enough to handle, peel away the blackened papery skin and discard. Remove any seeds and slice the soft flesh as desired, retaining as much of the roasting juices as possible.

PADRÓN PEPPERS: SOME ARE HOT; SOME ARE NOT…

* The Russian roulette of the pepper world, most Padrón peppers are mild and sweet, but one or two in ten are searingly hot. Appearances are no help at all; the only way to tell is to take a bite.

* Named after the area in northwestern Spain where they originated, Padrón peppers are most commonly fried whole and eaten as tapas. They are a great way to keep guests amused before their supper arrives! Give them a quick rinse and a pat dry. Heat a glug of olive oil in a wide frying pan over a medium–high heat until it's shimmering. Throw in the peppers – enough to make a single layer in the pan – and fry, tossing frequently, until softened, blistered and blackened in places. Serve immediately sprinkled with coarse sea salt for extra crunch, and a pinch of smoked paprika too if you like.

* For added interest you could cut a slit in each pepper and stuff it with a salty sheep's cheese, such as feta or goat's cheese, before frying (this counterbalances the very spicy ones).

* Or de-seed the peppers, slice them and use as a pizza topping. Store Padrón peppers in the fridge in the bag they came in and use within a week.

peppers

roast

Roasting peppers intensifies their flavour. Cut into chunks or slices, toss with olive oil and salt, spread over a lined baking sheet and roast at 200°C/Gas 6 until soft and caramelising in places, about 30 minutes. Check on them once or twice and give them a stir as they're prone to burning.

work well with...

* Anchovies
* Cheese – especially feta, goat's cheese, mozzarella
* Chilli and paprika
* Eggs
* Garlic
* Herbs – especially basil, marjoram, oregano
* Olives and olive oil
* Pork, lamb, chicken
* Tomatoes

IDEAS FOR ROAST PEPPERS

* Use as a pizza topping, or in a frittata, quiche or tart.

* Marinate overnight in a dressing of olive oil, sherry or balsamic vinegar, crushed garlic and chopped oregano. Mix with cherry tomatoes, torn mozzarella and basil for a salad.

* Combine with boiled Puy lentils, crumbled feta, fresh parsley and a dressing made with crushed garlic and balsamic vinegar for a heartier salad.

* Marinate in lemon juice, olive oil, crushed garlic, salt and pepper for at least 1 hour or overnight, then arrange on a platter with anchovy fillets, black olives and sliced boiled eggs.

* For soup, fry onions and garlic until soft, add a tin of tomatoes and simmer for 10 minutes or so. Add strips of peeled roast peppers and simmer for another 10 minutes. Blitz until very smooth, adding a dash of water if it's too thick, and brighten with a little balsamic, sherry or red wine vinegar. Serve with croutons and a drizzle of olive oil.

* For a dip: whizz a tin of cooked chickpeas, crushed garlic, lemon juice, tahini, chilli flakes and roast peppers in a food processor until smooth.

smoky quinoa-stuffed peppers
with sheep's cheese

quick & easy

vegetarian (if you use
vegetarian cheese)

SERVES 2

2 large or 3 smaller red
   peppers, cut in half
   lengthways, seeds and
   membranes removed
3 tbsp sunflower or light olive
   oil, for roasting and frying
1 onion, finely chopped
100g quinoa
1 garlic clove, finely chopped
   or crushed
¼–½ tsp smoked paprika,
   depending on how much
   you like it
1 x 400g tin chopped
   tomatoes, or use ripe,
   diced fresh tomatoes,
   peeled if you prefer, see
   page 224)
150g Wootton White or other
   salty vegetarian sheep's
   cheese
small bunch of parsley,
   finely chopped
salt and pepper

Quinoa is a seed first cultivated in South America that comes in three varieties: white, red and black – they each give a different flavour and look to dishes. Quinoa's low-key, slightly nutty taste absorbs spices well. Here we've used smoky sweet paprika and Wootton White, a British-made feta-style cheese – but use any salty sheep's cheese you like. Depending on the size of your peppers, you might have a little of the quinoa leftover to use in lunchbox salads. For other ideas for stuffing and cooking peppers in the same way, see pages 165 and 166.

Heat the oven to 200°C/Gas 6.

Put the peppers in a baking dish, toss with a little oil to coat, and season with salt and pepper. Roast in the oven for about 20–30 minutes, depending on size, while you make the filling.

Heat 2 tablespoons of oil in a medium-sized, heavy-bottomed saucepan. Add the onion. Fry on a low heat for 10 minutes, stirring now and then to stop it catching. Meanwhile, rinse the quinoa well in a sieve under cold water. After the 10 minutes, add the garlic and quinoa to the onion. Cook, stirring, for 2 minutes.

Add the smoked paprika, tomatoes and half a tinful of water. Season with salt and pepper. Bring the pan to a low boil, then cook for 15 minutes, stirring regularly. Keep a good eye on the liquid and the heat; you want the quinoa to absorb the liquid so you're left at the end with a risotto-like consistency, but not for the pan to boil dry – add a splash more water if needed.

Once the quinoa has cooked, remove from the heat. Take the peppers out of the oven, fill their cavities with the quinoa mixture and return them to the oven for 5 minutes to warm through. Remove the dish from the oven. Divide the peppers between serving plates, crumble over some of the cheese and scatter over the parsley.

Piedmontese peppers

a bit fancy

vegan

SERVES 4-6
AS A MAIN COURSE,
MORE AS A STARTER

2 tbsp capers
6 red peppers
olive oil
9 tomatoes
24 pitted black olives, halved
4 large or 6 small garlic
   cloves, thinly sliced
20g basil
salt and pepper

For the couscous (optional)
200g couscous
2 x 400g tins of chickpeas
zest and juice of ½ lemon,
   more to taste
2 tbsp extra virgin olive oil

The traditional non-vegetarian version of this stuffed pepper dish, named after the Piedmont region in northern Italy, uses anchovies; here we've substituted capers for saltiness, but if you're not vegetarian, use anchovies instead (or as well). Shred basil just before you need to use it; once the leaves are cut or torn, they blacken quickly. You can make the dish into a main course by serving it with the couscous to mop up any juices, or just serve the peppers with bread.

Heat the oven to 200°C/Gas 6. If you are using capers in brine, drain, put in a small bowl, cover with cold water and leave to soak for 15 minutes. (Capers in oil don't need soaking; just drain them.)

Cut the peppers in half lengthways, keeping the stalks intact if there are any left on. Remove the seeds and lay the pepper halves cut-side up on a lightly oiled roasting tray.

To peel the tomatoes, cut a small cross in the skin at the base of each tomato. Put them in a heatproof bowl or pan, cover with boiling water and leave for about 1 minute, just until you see the skins starting to peel away, then drain and plunge into the bowl of cold water. Drain again and slip the skins off. Cut into quarters and place three quarters in each pepper half.

Tuck the capers, olives and garlic slices in among the tomatoes. Spoon a dessertspoon of oil into each pepper and season with salt and pepper. Roast for about 50 minutes, until very tender and starting to caramelise at the edges.

Meanwhile, if you're making the couscous, pour it into a heatproof bowl and cover with boiling water and a little olive oil (this prevents the grains from sticking together). Leave the couscous to stand until the peppers are ready.

Drain the chickpeas and rinse well in a colander under cold running water. Leave to drain.

When the peppers are cooked, remove from the oven. Fluff the couscous with a fork and stir in the chickpeas. Add the lemon zest and juice, the extra virgin olive oil, salt and pepper to season. Taste and add more lemon juice or seasoning to taste. Divide between two serving plates, with the peppers on top, drizzled with any juices from the roasting tin and garnished with shredded basil leaves.

OTHER IDEAS FOR STUFFING PEPPERS

* Fry onion, garlic and a punnet of sliced mushrooms. Stir through a couple of handfuls of cooked pearl barley or spelt and mix with a good handful of chopped parsley. Add a little leftover roast chicken if you like.

* Use leftover chilli con carne, or a vegetarian equivalent, as a stuffing.

* Fry onion and garlic, then add minced pork or crumbled sausage meat and chopped rosemary and fry for a further 15 minutes or so. Add a diced tomato and fry for another 5 minutes. Stuff the peppers, sprinkle over some grated Parmesan or Cheddar and bake until golden.

* You could use halved cherry tomatoes instead of the wedges of tomatoes (don't bother peeling them).

romesco sauce

long, slow cook

vegan

freezable

SERVES 4-6

1 whole head of garlic
olive oil
4 red peppers
50g whole hazelnuts
150g blanched almonds
1 tsp paprika
½ tsp smoked paprika
2 dried chillies, crumbled,
   or a good pinch or two
   of chilli flakes
1 tsp dried mint
2 tsp red wine vinegar,
   plus a little more to taste
salt and pepper

Spanish in origin, a romesco sauce is a good way to spice
up all sorts of veg. Try it with roasted or boiled new or salad
potatoes or drizzle over cooked leeks or spring and summer
greens. Traditionally it often contains breadcrumbs to thicken
it, but this version is gluten-free. It can be made a little ahead
and will keep in the fridge for a couple of days.

Heat the oven to 200°C/Gas 6.

Slice the top off the garlic bulb to reveal the tips of the cloves.
Drizzle with a little olive oil and wrap in foil. Put the peppers
in a baking dish without any oil. Put the garlic on a baking sheet
and roast both in the oven for 45 minutes, turning the peppers
once during cooking, until the peppers skins are blackened
and the garlic is soft.

Meanwhile, put the hazelnuts on a separate baking sheet and
roast in the oven until the skins start to darken, about 10–12
minutes. (Watch them closely as they can quickly go from toasted
to burned.) Remove and leave to cool slightly, then rub them
in a clean tea towel to remove the skins.

Put the almonds in a dry frying pan and heat gently, stirring now
and then, until golden. Remove from the heat and leave to cool.

Once cooked, remove the peppers and garlic from the oven.
Put the peppers into a bowl and cover with a plate or cling film
and leave for a few minutes, until cool enough to handle, then
peel off the skins.

Put the almonds, hazelnuts, peppers, both sorts of paprika, dried
chilli, dried mint and vinegar in a food processor with a good pinch
of salt. Open up the garlic and squeeze in the soft roasted cloves.
Blitz, adding enough olive oil to make a thick sauce. Taste and
add more vinegar, seasoning or oil as necessary.

summer vegetable paella
with saffron and lemon

vegan

A vegetarian adaptation of the traditional Spanish dish, paella rice is readily available but use short-grain brown or Arborio if you can't find it. Saffron threads give the dish its unique flavour.

SERVES 2

sunflower or light olive oil, for frying

1 onion, finely diced

2 garlic cloves, finely chopped, grated or crushed

1 red pepper, deseeded and cut into 5mm-thick slices

1 yellow pepper, deseeded and cut into 5mm-thick slices

200g paella rice – calasparra paella rice if you can get it (or see above)

100g mushrooms, finely sliced

3 tomatoes, diced

¼ tsp smoked paprika

¼ tsp paprika

2 pinches of saffron threads

1 litre of good veg stock

100g green beans or sugar snaps, or a mixture of both (if using beans, top, tail and chop into thirds)

good handful of parsley, chopped

1 lemon, cut into wedges

salt and pepper

Heat 2 tablespoons of oil in a heavy-bottomed paella pan or large frying pan or flameproof casserole. Add the onion and fry gently on a low heat for 10 minutes, stirring now and then.

Add the garlic and peppers to the onion and stir for 2 minutes. Add the rice, mushrooms, tomatoes, both types of paprika and saffron. Pour in three quarters of the stock and season with salt and pepper. Bring to a gentle simmer and cook for 30 minutes, stirring occasionally. Keep an eye on the liquid and top up with a little more stock or water as needed (you might not need it all). The paella shouldn't be sloppy at the end so add liquid sparingly during the last 10 minutes.

While the paella is cooking, boil the green beans for 3 minutes, then refresh them in a bowl of very cold water. If you are using sugar snaps, you can simply throw them in raw towards the end of cooking (see below).

After 30 minutes of cooking, check the rice is tender and cook a little longer if needed. If there is any excess liquid, turn up the heat and stir to boil it off. Then cook very gently without stirring, to create a crust on the bottom (it's not very easy to achieve without a proper paella pan, though). Stir in the beans and parsley. Turn off the heat and leave to stand for 2 minutes, then check the seasoning and serve with wedges of lemon.

VARIATION
You can use any sort of green beans in this; try double-podded broad beans (see page 60), sliced runners or flat green beans.

patatas a lo pobre

quick & easy

vegan

SERVES 4

5 tbsp olive oil

500–600g waxy potatoes,
  peeled and thickly sliced

2 onions, diced

2 red or green peppers,
  deseeded and thickly sliced

4 garlic cloves, roughly
  chopped

2 bay leaves

handful of parsley, chopped

1 tsp sherry or red
  wine vinegar

salt and pepper

Meaning 'poor man's potatoes', this rustic Andalusian dish of potatoes slowly fried in oil is hearty and filling. It is enough for a vegetarian main course on its own, served with a crisp green salad, but could also accompany any simply-cooked chicken or steak as an alternative to roast potatoes or fries. Use a firm, waxy potato; floury ones will just collapse in the pan.

Warm the oil in a large heavy-bottomed pan – a big frying pan or wok is ideal. Add the potatoes and onions and cook on a low heat, stirring occasionally, for 10 minutes.

Add the peppers, garlic, bay leaves and some salt and pepper and continue cooking for another 10–20 minutes, until all the vegetables are soft. The potatoes may break up a little but that's fine. Covering the pan will speed up the cooking. If it looks like it is catching, add a splash of water to help it along.

Once everything is cooked, drain off any excess oil if you like and taste for seasoning. Stir in the parsley and sprinkle with the vinegar before serving.

lamb, red pepper and coconut curry

long slow cook

freezable

SERVES 2

250g diced lamb shoulder
sunflower or light olive
    oil, for frying (or try
    coconut oil)
1 onion, finely sliced
2 garlic cloves, finely
    chopped, crushed
    or grated
3cm piece of fresh ginger,
    peeled and finely grated
1 red pepper, deseeded
    and thinly sliced
1 red chilli, deseeded and
    finely chopped (for more
    heat, leave the seeds in)
1 tsp ground cumin
2 bay leaves
2 star anise
1 cinnamon stick
1 x 400ml tin coconut milk
salt and pepper

Star anise is a pretty, star-shaped spice that adds a fragrant, aniseed flavour. It's great in curries or added to rice for a little extra flavour. You can buy packs of whole ones, but you'll often pay a little more for those. It's fine just to use broken up pieces – the equivalent of 2 whole ones. Cinnamon can be overpowering if strong, and whole sticks can vary in size, so taste at intervals and fish it out once you've got enough of the flavour. Serve with basmati rice.

Season the lamb with salt and pepper. Heat 2 tablespoons of oil in a large, heavy-bottomed saucepan. Add the lamb and fry on a high heat, turning the meat every so often, until sealed and browned all over. Make sure there is space between the pieces – cook in a couple of batches if need be. Transfer the meat to a plate.

Lower the heat and add a splash more oil. Fry the onion on a low heat for 10 minutes, stirring now and then to stop it catching. If it does start to catch, add a splash of water, stir and turn the heat down further. Add the garlic and ginger and fry, stirring often, for a further 2 minutes.

Return the lamb to the pan, along with the pepper, chilli and cumin. Stir for a minute. Add the bay leaves, star anise and cinnamon stick. Stir the coconut milk in the can then pour that in too. Season, bring the pan to a simmer and cook for about 2 hours, or until the lamb is tender. Check halfway through and remove the cinnamon stick if the flavour is strong enough; too much cooking and it can overpower the dish. Keep an eye on the liquid and top up if needed.

Check the lamb is tender and that you're happy with the seasoning, then lift out the star anise, cinnamon and bay leaves before serving.

warm roasted pepper and lentil salad with olives and halloumi

vegetarian, vegan if you
leave out the halloumi

SERVES 2

4 red peppers

2 tbsp sunflower or
    light olive oil

1 small red onion,
    finely diced

2 carrots, finely diced

2 celery sticks, finely diced

2 garlic cloves, finely
    chopped, grated or
    crushed

100g Puy-style lentils, rinsed
    in a sieve under cold water

1 bay leaf

¼ tsp dried oregano

¼ tsp ground cumin

¼ tsp dried mint

1 tbsp red wine vinegar

100g pitted black olives

1 pack (150–200g) halloumi,
    cut into 1–2cm-thick slices

small glug of extra virgin
    olive oil

50g watercress

small handful of chopped
    fresh mint and/or
    parsley, to garnish

salt and pepper

Halloumi is a very useful cheese to have in your fridge. It gives vegetarian dishes a salty hit and its firm texture means it stands up to frying or grilling, which brings out the flavour. If you'd prefer to make the dish vegan, it can stand up without the halloumi.

As well as adding peppery flavour to salads, watercress wilts into soups, stews and warm salads too, giving extra nutrients.

Char and peel the peppers as described on page 158. While they're cooking, heat the oil in a large saucepan. Add the onion, carrot and celery and fry on a low heat for 15 minutes, stirring now and then. If they look as if they might catch at any point, add a splash of water. Once softened, add the garlic and cook, stirring, for 2 minutes.

Add the lentils, bay leaf, oregano, cumin, mint and 300ml water. Bring to the boil and simmer for 20–25 minutes, until the lentils are tender. Keep an eye on the liquid towards the end and top up with a little extra water as needed. Almost all the liquid should have been absorbed by the end of cooking. Once done, remove from the heat if the peppers aren't quite ready.

Roughly chop the peppers into strips and stir them into the lentils with the vinegar and olives. Remove the bay leaf and season to taste. Set aside while you fry the halloumi.

Heat a dry non-stick frying pan, add the halloumi slices and fry for about 2 minutes on each side, until golden. Gently warm the lentils if needed, then stir in the watercress and extra virgin olive oil and serve with the halloumi slices on top, scattered with the fresh herbs.

VARIATION
Instead of halloumi, crumble over some feta or goat's cheese.

spinach
and
chard
june to november

We plant out the first spinach and chard in March for picking from June (or late April on our French farm). Successional sowings allow harvest right into early winter when the first hard frost and gales damage the leaves enough to make sorting the good from the bad too time consuming. Commercially we only pick the crop once but if you have even a small garden and are wanting a steady source of greens, both chard and spinach beet lend themselves well to repeat 'cut and come again' cropping. Either cut the whole plants down to the ground or, to maximise output, pick individual leaves. Early sowings might run to seed but from June you can be picking right through the summer, autumn and, with care, patience and a bit of sorting, even into the following spring.

Spinach is an excellent source of iron, and contains a treasure-trove of other nutritional wonders, including vitamin K, vitamin A, vitamin C and folic acid. It is also a good source of manganese, magnesium and vitamin B2. Chard, too, is high in vitamins A, K, and C and is also rich in minerals, dietary fibre and protein.

Guy

spinach and chard

identifying

We grow two types of spinach: dark green, true spinach, with spade-shaped leaves and thin, tender leaf stalks, and the more robust, stronger flavoured, paler green perpetual spinach beet.

TRUE SPINACH is more tender and appears in the boxes in late summer and early autumn. It has a disconcerting way of collapsing in the pan, so you tend to need a lot of it.

SPINACH BEET (or perpetual spinach) is more hardy and has a longer season, appearing in veg boxes around the end of April or early May right through to autumn and early winter. For cooking it is similar to chard but the leaf ribs tend to be tougher and, at least for larger leaves, are often best discarded.

CHARD has large, succulent green leaves with thicker, fleshy stems, which can be white (Swiss chard), reddish (ruby chard, bull's bloods, etc.), yellow or a mix of all three (rainbow chard). In the summer, we send out mostly loose-leaved bags of chard, but occasionally whole heads. Swiss chard, with its white, fleshy leaf mid ribs, is invariably the best. Strip the green from the fleshy ribs and cut crosswise; they take a bit more cooking than the greens.

storage

Keep leafy greens such as spinach and chard in their plastic bag in the fridge. Use fairly quickly, within a few days, though chard will usually keep a little longer than spinach.

prep

Chard leaves and stalks cook quite differently, so need separating. With spinach, just snap off and discard any larger, tougher stalks. Wash both well to remove any grit and dirt – it's best to put them in a large bowl of water and let any dirt sink to the bottom.

eating spinach and chard raw

Baby spinach and chard leaves are delicious raw tossed into a mixed green leaf salad.

> **TIP**
> If a recipe calls for chard leaves but not their stems, go ahead and blanch the stems too, then refrigerate or freeze them for making a cheesy gratin another day. Adding a pinch of bicarbonate of soda to the water stops white stems turning an unattractive grey and helps rainbow chard stems maintain their vibrant pink, red and yellow hues.

cooking

Chard and spinach are both quick and easy to cook and need very little extra in the way of flavouring.

fast cook

Wash well, then tear or slice spinach or chard leaves into ribbons, or leave them whole if small. Cook them quickly in a hot pan with a dash of heated oil or butter and the water still clinging to them. Keep them moving in the pan; they should wilt within moments. Season to taste. If you like, add some chopped garlic (and chilli or anchovy depending on your tastes) to the hot fat and fry it for a couple of minutes before adding the spinach or chard. A dash of lemon juice at the very end is a great lift but don't be tempted to add it earlier or the acid will turn the green leaves brown.

Finely sliced raw chard stems can be added to a stir-fry along with other quick-cooking vegetables. Or blanch the stems as described on page 176 then slice or dice them finely and add them to your fast-cooked chard leaves (see above) just to heat through.

FLAVOUR ADDITIONS FOR WILTED SPINACH

Try adding some of the following to 250g wilted spinach or chard:

* A grating of nutmeg to your taste along with the salt and pepper. At the last minute add a good squeeze of lemon juice, mix well and serve immediately.

* Gently fry 2 finely chopped garlic cloves in 20g butter for a few minutes until fragrant but not burning. Add the spinach/chard, turn up the heat and wilt. Pour in 50ml double cream and bubble for a few minutes, then season to taste.

* Fry 1 very finely chopped shallot, 1 teaspoon grated fresh ginger, a crushed garlic clove and ½ finely chopped red chilli in 1 tablespoon of sesame oil for 3 minutes. Add the spinach/chard and a pinch of salt and wilt for a few minutes. Dress with soy sauce, to taste.

spinach and chard

slow braise

Slow-cooked chard will lose its bright colour, but the flavour is just as good. Slice the stems finely and the leaves into 2cm-wide ribbons. Heat a little oil or butter in a pan and fry a few aromatics – onion, garlic, chilli, spices – then mix in the chard and fry for a few minutes more. Add water or stock to barely cover and continue to simmer over low–medium heat, covered, for about 10–20 minutes, until tender. Remove the lid towards the end of cooking to boil off excess water, and finish with some lemon juice or vinegar to brighten the flavour. For a heartier dish, include a tin of chickpeas or beans, or try one of our recipes on pages 184–185.

blanch and squeeze

Pre-blanching works well for some recipes, particularly where you want to remove any excess liquid first, to prevent the green leaves leeching their colour into your dish. For spinach, blanch the leaves for 1–2 minutes, just enough to wilt them. For chard, blanch the stems and leaves separately in boiling salted water until tender; they'll need approximately 6–10 and 2–3 minutes respectively. Plunge them into a bowl of ice-cold water to cool, then drain. The idea is to stop the cooking and cool the leaves quickly so that they retain their bright colour. Squeeze the leaves to remove excess water.

They are now ready to be used in all manner of ways:

* reheat in a pan with oil or butter and flavourings such as garlic, chilli and spices.

* cover with cream, cheese and breadcrumbs for a gratin.

* pile on toast rubbed with garlic and drizzle with good-quality olive oil.

* use in a lasagne, with or without meat.

* whizz chard stems into a hummus along with tahini, garlic, lemon juice and olive oil.

FREEZING

Chard and spinach are a great freezer staple. Once blanched and squeezed, they can be frozen (chopped first or as whole leaves) in portion-size balls of goodness. If you have a glut from your veg box or garden, batch cook and freeze for later use.

work well with...

* Asian flavourings – chilli, ginger, sesame, soy sauce
* Cheese – especially ricotta and feta, also hard cheeses
* Dairy – butter, cream, crème fraîche
* Dried fruit – raisins and currants
* Garlic
* Lemon juice and preserved lemon rind
* Mustard
* Olives and olive oil
* Pork – bacon, chorizo, ham
* Spices – cayenne, chilli, mace, nutmeg, paprika

pasta with spinach, walnut and basil pesto

quick & easy

vegetarian (if you use
vegetarian cheese)

freezable

SERVES 4

30g walnut pieces

20g pine nuts

400g dried pasta (any type;
   use your preferred shape)

2 garlic cloves

¼ tsp freshly grated nutmeg

zest of ½ and juice
   of 1 lemon

200g spinach, washed
   well, any larger, tough
   stalks removed

100g Parmesan or vegetarian
   alternative, grated

50g basil

100ml olive oil, more
   if needed

salt and pepper

Make sure when using any nuts that they are fresh – they turn stale quickly, even within their best before date, particularly once the pack is opened so buy small amounts, as and when you need them. If you aren't that tolerant to wheat, try a spelt pasta, which can be easier to digest even though still a grain, or for a gluten-free option, rice pastas are readily available. If you have any leftover pesto, it will keep in the fridge for a few days, covered with a layer of oil, or freeze it.

Stir the walnut pieces in a dry frying pan on a low heat for a minute or so, to lightly toast them. Repeat with the pine nuts, keeping a good eye on them as they catch and burn easily.

Add the pasta to a large pan of boiling salted water and cook according to the packet instructions.

While the pasta cooks, put the walnuts, pine nuts, garlic, nutmeg, lemon zest and juice, spinach, half the Parmesan and all but a few leaves of the basil in a food processor. Blitz, gradually pouring in oil until the mixture forms a rough paste. Season with salt and pepper to taste.

Drain the pasta, reserving a ladle of the cooking water, then toss with enough pesto to coat, adding a little of the reserved water to thin the sauce if needed. Stir in the remaining Parmesan, check the seasoning and serve, garnished with the reserved basil leaves.

VARIATION
Swap the walnuts for almonds or hazelnuts. For a complete change, instead of pasta try slicing courgettes lengthways into 0.5cm strips, then into thin noodle-like strands instead. Toss them raw into the pesto, or warm them both through so the courgettes soften and wilt a little.

braised spinach or chard with...

Braising allows you to add different
flavours to your greens. These are just
a few of our favourites. With the addition
of some couscous, boiled rice or quinoa,
you can make a simple supper in no time.

anchovies, tomatoes and raisins

quick & easy

SERVES 2

olive oil
1 small onion, finely sliced
4 salted anchovy fillets
2 fresh tomatoes, chopped
1 garlic clove, finely chopped
25g raisins, chopped
1 tbsp red wine vinegar
250g spinach or chard

Heat a little olive oil gently in a large
pan, add the onion and fry over a low
heat for 5 minutes. Add the anchovies,
tomatoes, garlic, raisins and vinegar
and cook for a further 5 minutes until
most of the vinegar has evaporated and
plumped up the raisins. Add the spinach
or chard and a dash of water, lower the
heat and cook for 15 minutes.

chickpeas and coconut

quick & easy

vegan

SERVES 2

splash of sunflower or
  light olive oil, for frying
½ tbsp curry powder
200ml coconut milk
250g spinach or chard
½ x 400g tin chickpeas, rinsed
salt and black pepper

Heat a little oil, add the curry powder
and fry gently for 30 seconds to release
the flavour.

Pour in the coconut milk and bring to
a simmer. Stir in the spinach or chard,
add the chickpeas and season well. Loosely
cover and cook gently for 20 minutes until
the coconut milk has reduced and thickened.

onions and egg

quick & easy

vegetarian (if you use a
vegetarian alternative
to Parmesan)

SERVES 2

2 large onions, sliced
1 garlic clove, finely chopped
250g spinach or chard
2 eggs
2 tbsp grated Parmesan (optional)
hot buttered toast, to serve

In a shallow casserole or lidded frying pan
gently fry the onions in oil for 25 minutes,
stirring occasionally until very soft and
slightly coloured. Add the garlic and spinach
or chard and cook for 10 minutes until most
of the liquid has disappeared.

Make two nest-like holes in the spinach/
chard and crack an egg into each one. Pop on
the lid and cook for about 5 minutes until the
whites have set and the yolks remain runny.

Grate over some Parmesan and serve
with hot buttered toast.

spinach, olive and feta tart

a bit fancy

vegetarian (if you use
vegetarian cheese)

This is a really adaptable recipe and a great crowd-pleaser.
Using the pastry case as your base, you can vary the fillings
as much as you like – see our list of suggestions overleaf.
Use a good ready-made shortcrust to save time if you prefer.

SERVES 6–8

For the pastry
250g plain flour, plus a little
    extra for rolling out
150g cold unsalted butter,
    diced, plus a little extra
    for greasing the tart tin
¼ tsp fine sea salt
1 large egg, yolk and
    white separated

For the filling
small knob of butter
splash of oil, for frying
1 large onion, finely diced
300g spinach, leaves stripped
    from their stalks
3 large eggs
200ml crème fraîche
200g feta
100g pitted black olives
1 tbsp chopped dill leaves,
    or 1 tsp dried dill
salt and pepper

To make the pastry, put the flour, butter and salt in a food
processor and blitz until it looks like breadcrumbs. Add the egg
yolk and pulse, adding just enough cold water so that the pastry
starts to come together in a ball. Roll the pastry into a smooth
ball, wrap in cling film and chill in the fridge for at least an hour.

Meanwhile, melt a knob of butter with a splash of oil in a small
frying pan. Add the onion and fry gently for 10 minutes, until
soft and translucent. Remove from the heat and leave to cool.

Boil or steam the spinach leaves for 2–3 minutes, until wilted.
Drain and refresh in a bowl of ice-cold water. Once cooled,
drain again and squeeze the spinach really well several times
to get rid of any excess liquid. Roughly chop the leaves.

Heat the oven to 180°C/Gas 4. Lightly flour a work surface
and rolling pin. Lightly grease a 23cm tart tin with butter.

Roll out the pastry to a rough circle, a little bigger than needed
to line the tin. Lay the pastry in the tin, pressing it into all the
crevices. Trim any overhanging pastry. Chill the pastry in the
fridge for a further 5 minutes. Put a baking sheet in the oven.

Line the pastry case with baking parchment and fill with baking
beans or dried, uncooked pulses or rice, making sure all the
crevices are filled so the pastry doesn't rise. Place the tin on the hot
baking sheet and bake for 15 minutes. Lift out the paper and beans,
and bake for a further 10 minutes. Remove from the oven, brush
lightly with just enough egg white to coat and seal the base (this
helps prevent a soggy pastry bottom), then leave to cool completely.

spinach, olive and feta tart *continued*

Once the pastry has cooled, beat the eggs for the filling in a large bowl. Stir in the crème fraîche and crumble in the feta. Add the spinach, onion, dill and half the olives. Season with salt and pepper. Gently combine then pour the mixture into the pastry case. Press the rest of the olives into the top so they're visible once baked. Bake for about 30 minutes, until the filling has just set.

Remove and leave to cool to just warm or room temperature before cutting into slices to serve.

VARIATIONS

* Use chard leaves or spring or summer greens instead of spinach. To include chard stems, chop them small and fry along with the onion. In winter, substitute with shredded kale or even cabbage.

* Try other veg, such as fried courgette, asparagus or beans.

* Add a few sun-dried tomatoes with the olives.

* Vary the herbs – try thyme, basil, oregano or marjoram.

* Add some garlic – fry some shredded wet garlic with the onion, or add some shredded wild garlic leaves just before baking.

* Use chopped spring onions instead of onions (these need minimal frying).

* Ring the changes with the cheese – try blue cheese, Cheddar, Parmesan, or simply use up what you have in your fridge.

----

chard and rosemary gratin

quick & easy

vegetarian (if you use a
vegetarian cheese)

SERVES 2 AS A MAIN,
4 AS A SIDE

knob (approx. 25g) of butter
sunflower or light olive oil,
    for frying
1 large onion (or leek),
    finely sliced
1 large rosemary sprig,
    leaves very finely chopped
1 head of Swiss chard, or
    300g loose chard leaves,
    leaves and stalks separated
1 large or 2 small garlic
    cloves, finely chopped
    or crushed
1 tbsp plain flour
125ml crème fraîche
small handful of finely
    grated Parmesan
salt and pepper

If you've got a whole head of Swiss chard or loose leaves with fat stalks, use the whole thing and cook the stalks too. If you've got leaves with very skinny, stringy stalks, these aren't worth bothering with; remove and discard them and use a few more leaves instead. Serve this as a vegetarian main course, accompanied by crusty bread, boiled potatoes or rice, or alongside a roast or quick grilled lamb chops.

Heat the oven to 190°C/Gas 5.

Heat the butter and a splash of oil in a frying pan over a low heat. Add the onion and rosemary and fry, stirring, for 10 minutes, until soft and translucent.

Meanwhile, chop the chard stalks (if using) into 2cm pieces and boil for 5 minutes in a large pan of salted water. Add the chard leaves and boil for a further 2–3 minutes. Drain and add both stalks and leaves to the onion, along with the garlic and flour. Fry gently, stirring often, for 2 minutes.

Add the crème fraîche, season with salt and pepper and stir for 2 minutes. Transfer the mixture to a small gratin dish. Sprinkle over the cheese. Cook for 20–25 minutes, until the cheese is golden and the gratin bubbling.

frying-pan spinach soufflé

quick & easy

SERVES 2

300g spinach, washed, leaves
   stripped from their stalks
4 eggs
¼ tsp ground nutmeg
1 good tsp wholegrain
   mustard
75g grated Cheddar
sunflower or light olive oil,
   for frying
salt and pepper

The word soufflé seems to strike fear into the hearts of even competent cooks, but this version is simple and accommodating. All you're looking for is to get the eggs to rise slightly, then crisp a little on top, like a puffy omelette. You need a smallish frying pan which can go in the oven - 21-23cm in diameter. The two things to get right with any form of soufflé are to whisk your egg whites until you can tip the bowl over your head without them falling out (really!) and to fold them in gently to keep as much air in the mixture as possible.

Heat your oven to 210°C/Gas 6. Cook the spinach in a pan of boiling water for 1–2 minutes, until wilted. Drain and refresh in a bowl of cold water, then drain again. Wring it out with your hands to remove excess water, then roughly chop the leaves.

Separate the egg whites and yolks into 2 bowls. Whisk the egg whites until they form firm but soft peaks – an electric whisk makes life easier. Lightly beat the egg yolks together. Add the spinach to the yolks, then add the nutmeg, mustard and three quarters of the cheese. Season with salt and pepper.

Take a spoonful of the egg white and stir it into the egg yolk mixture, then very gently fold in the rest.

Pour 1 tablespoon of oil into a 21–23cm frying pan. Wipe the base and sides with kitchen paper to coat it. Heat the oil gently, then tip in the egg mix and tip the pan from side to side to cover it.

Sprinkle over the remaining cheese. Transfer the pan to the oven for 10 minutes, until the mixture has risen and is fluffy and slightly golden from the melted cheese on top. Cut in half or wedges to serve.

spring greens

january to july

Spring greens are winter-hardy cabbages sown in July or August and harvested when green vegetables are scarce (January to April) as immature, loose heads without hearts. In a good year they bring a youthful freshness when winter veg is getting dull and tired. Every season is different. At their best, spring greens can be sweet and tender but after a hard winter, they can verge on tough and bitter (let's say 'robust') and need more cooking; you will get a pretty good idea when you are chopping them.

In the calendar of cabbages, spring greens are closely followed in June by 'summer greens', the first, fast-growing cabbage, which would mature into a hearted pointed hispi cabbage if they were given the chance. Boiled or steamed they need very little cooking. I can eat mountains of them on their own, but they're even better with butter and a squeeze of lemon. You will find spring greens in your veg box most weeks throughout May and June.

Guy

spring greens

storage

Spring greens are best kept in a plastic bag in the fridge and eaten within three or four days.

prep

You can give whole leaves a quick rinse under the cold tap, but it is generally better to cut them up first (see below), stand them in a big bowl of water for a few minutes, then lift them out with your hands or a strainer, leaving the dirt at the bottom of the bowl.

For quick frying, or adding to soups or stews, shred them finely: cut out the tough central ribs, stack the leaves in a pile, roll up into a fat cigar and then slice crossways to the thickness required for your recipe.

eating spring and summer greens raw

Like other cabbages, spring greens can be sliced up finely for a coleslaw. Try a mustardy vinaigrette (see page 198) or take inspiration from South East Asia (see page 201).

cooking

Greens cook quickly, making them an easy and versatile weeknight veg that can be boiled, fried or stirred into a pot of soup or stew. Cooking times do vary: greens will need a few extra minutes at the beginning of the season – they start out hardy and soften as the weather warms, finally becoming 'summer greens'. When searching for inspiration for spring greens, consider any recipe that calls for cabbage or kale, with which they are largely interchangeable.

fry

Shred the greens finely so that they cook quickly. Heat butter or oil in a wide frying pan, add some aromatics if you like (garlic is very good), then follow 30 seconds or so later with the greens, taking care not to burn the garlic. Fry over medium heat for just a few minutes, stirring and tossing frequently, until the greens are just tender.

Fried greens are particularly good with Indian flavours – e.g. chilli, ginger, garlic, mustard seeds and other Indian spices in at the beginning, with perhaps a squeeze of lemon at the end. They also work well with Chinese flavours – garlic, chilli and ginger in at the beginning, then sliced spring onions if you have any, soy and/or oyster sauce, rice wine and sesame oil when the greens are nearly done.

blanch

It's sometimes easier to cut up the leaves first, but for some recipes blanching the leaves whole and chopping them afterwards is a better way to prepare them.

Bring a pot of salted water to a boil, add the greens and boil until tender, about 2–6 minutes depending on toughness. Strain and refresh in a bowl of cold water to stop the cooking and fix the bright green colour, then drain again, thoroughly. Serve immediately while still warm, or cool fast and reheat later in a frying pan with some butter or oil.

simmer

Add shredded greens to a soup or stew and let them simmer with the other ingredients until tender, usually 5–10 minutes depending on the contents of the pot and on how finely they're sliced. Try adding them to:

* a spring or early summer minestrone full of green goodness – courgettes, peas, asparagus etc. (see page 42).

* a pot of beans, chickpeas or lentils. Some bacon or chorizo is a particularly good match here.

* a pot of boiling pasta a few minutes before the pasta will be done. You need to judge the timing right, but it saves using two pans. Drain the pasta and greens and return to the warm pan to toss with butter, olive oil or cream, and plenty of Parmesan and black pepper.

* a hearty meaty stew, to add a touch of spring. You could also add some wild garlic leaves right at the end (allowing just enough time for them to wilt).

IDEAS FOR BLANCHED GREENS

* Dress simply with butter, pepper, sea salt and a squeeze of lemon or with one of our ideas for dressings overleaf.

* Indulge with a rich hollandaise sauce.

* Drizzle with romesco sauce (see page 167).

* Mix with pasta, along with olive oil, chilli flakes and grated Parmesan. You could also try adding a little chopped anchovy and/or lemon zest.

* Fold into a risotto when the rice is nearly cooked (see page 37).

spring greens

work well with...

* Alliums – garlic, leeks, onions, spring onions, wild garlic
* Asian spices and flavourings
* Butter
* Cheese – fresh cheeses and hard cheeses
* Fish and shellfish
* Lemon juice and zest
* Lentils
* Mustard and mustard seeds
* Nuts and seeds, especially coconut, peanuts, pine nuts, sesame seeds
* Pork in all forms

KEEPING GREENS GREEN

For bright green greens – be they spring greens, beans, broccoli, chard or kale – the secret is to cook them quickly and then stop the cooking. Bring plenty of water to a rolling boil so that it returns quickly to the boil when you add the veg, then strain as soon as they are tender. (You can add a pinch of baking soda, but too much will make your veg mushy.) Once cooked, cool green veg fast so they stop cooking and keep their colour: spread them over a tea towel or plunge them into very cold water.

dressings for spring and summer greens

Each of the following recipes makes enough to use on 300-400g of cooked greens. Most of these dressings can also be used to liven up summer carrots, kohlrabi, potatoes, purple sprouting broccoli and other greens in winter.

quick & easy

vegetarian

lemon butter

good knob of butter, about 25g or so
finely grated zest and juice of ½ lemon
salt and black pepper

Melt the butter, then squeeze in the lemon juice and season well with salt and pepper. Toss in your cooked greens. Serve immediately, sprinkled with the zest.

chilli and parsley oil

small handful of parsley leaves, finely chopped
1 large garlic clove, crushed
1 red chilli, deseeded and finely chopped
100ml good olive or rapeseed oil
salt and black pepper

Mix everything together in a small bowl or shake in a jam jar. Season with salt and pepper to taste.

mustard and tarragon dressing

2 tsp wholegrain mustard
4 tbsp olive oil
1 tbsp finely chopped tarragon leaves
    (or chervil for a milder flavour)
a squeeze of lemon juice
salt and black pepper

Whisk the mustard and oil together in a small bowl. Add the tarragon, season with salt and pepper and stir in a little lemon juice to taste.

tahini and lemon dressing

2 tbsp light tahini
2 tbsp plain yoghurt
1 garlic clove, crushed or finely chopped
2 tbsp extra virgin olive oil
juice of 1 lemon, to taste
salt and freshly ground black pepper

Stir together the tahini and yoghurt to make a smooth paste. Whisk in the remaining ingredients, gradually adding a few tablespoons of water to get the consistency of pouring cream. Season with salt and pepper.

gremolata

2 garlic cloves, finely chopped
finely grated zest from 2 small lemons
2 tbsp chopped parsley leaves
salt and black pepper

Mix the garlic, lemon zest and parsley in a bowl and add a tiny squeeze of lemon juice. Season with salt and pepper.

bagna cauda

8 garlic cloves
200ml milk
10 tinned anchovy fillets
100g butter, softened
olive oil
black pepper

Simmer the garlic in a pan with the milk until soft. Transfer to a food processor with the anchovies and blitz until smooth. Gradually add the butter, then drizzle in enough oil to make a sloppy sauce. Season with freshly ground black pepper to taste (you probably won't need to add salt as the anchovies are salty). If the sauce splits, warm and whisk it gently in the pan again to bring it back together.

Drizzle over greens or use as a dip for other summer veg.

summer ribollita

vegetarian (if you use
vegetarian cheese)

This Italian pottage is a hearty meal in a bowl. Ribollita translates
as 'twice boiled', a reference to the fact that it is a stew born of
the thrifty practice of taking the leftovers from other meals and
creating a new one. We've adapted the traditional recipe to make
a more summery version.

SERVES 2

1 tbsp sunflower or
    light olive oil
2 celery sticks, finely diced
2 carrots, finely diced
200g new potatoes, scrubbed
    clean, cut into ½cm dice
2 garlic cloves, crushed
    or finely chopped
1 tsp ground fennel seeds
leaves from 3 thyme sprigs
½ red chilli, deseeded and
    finely chopped, or a pinch
    of dried chilli flakes
1 x 400g tin chopped
    tomatoes, or 400g ripe,
    skinned, chopped
    fresh tomatoes
1 bay leaf
1 x 400g tin cannellini beans
200g spring greens, tough
    ribs removed, leaves
    finely shredded
2 spring onions, finely sliced
2 handfuls of chunkily torn
    pieces of bread
handful of grated Parmesan
    (or vegetarian alternative)
pesto, to serve (see page 44)
salt and pepper

Heat 1 tablespoon of oil in a heavy-bottomed ovenproof
saucepan. Add the celery and carrots and fry on a low heat,
stirring occasionally, for 10 minutes. If they look like catching
at any point, add a splash of water.

Add the potatoes, garlic, fennel, thyme and chilli to the pan.
Cook for 2 minutes, stirring continuously, until everything
smells fragrant.

Add the tomatoes, bay leaf and cannellini beans, including
their liquid (it acts like a stock) and pour in enough water to
cover everything. Season, bring up to a simmer and cook
until everything is tender, about 20–25 minutes.

Heat the oven to 200°C/Gas 6. Add the spring greens to the
pan and cook for a further 5 minutes. Stir in the spring onions.

Press the chunks of bread on top of the stew. You want them
to soak up liquid but to stay at the top of the pan. Sprinkle the
cheese over and bake in the oven for about 10 minutes, until the
topping has coloured and crisped a little. Ladle into bowls and
serve with a spoonful of pesto on top.

VARIATIONS
* Use summer greens or shredded Hispi cabbage.
* In winter, swap for Savoy cabbage or kale.

miso-baked salmon with sesame spring greens and noodles

quick & easy

We haven't added any seasoning to the greens deliberately, as the miso and soy are salty (for more about miso see page 57), but if you like, add a touch of salt and pepper to suit your taste.

SERVES 2

2 salmon fillets
  (about 150–175g each)
oil for baking and frying,
  e.g. sunflower
1 tbsp brown rice miso paste
1 lime
200g brown rice noodles
2 tbsp sesame oil
200g spring greens, central
  ribs cut out, washed and
  finely shredded
2 spring onions, trimmed
  and finely sliced on
  the diagonal
1 large or 2 smaller garlic
  cloves, finely chopped,
  grated or crushed
1 red chilli, thinly sliced
  (remove the seeds if
  you prefer less heat)
3cm piece of fresh ginger,
  peeled and finely grated
  or sliced
1 tbsp soy sauce
2 tbsp sesame seeds
black pepper

Heat the oven to 200°C/Gas 6.

Put the salmon (skin side down if there is any on the fillet) in a lightly oiled baking dish.

In a small bowl, mix the miso with the juice from half the lime and a splash of water to thin it slightly. Spread it over the top of the salmon, then season with pepper. Put the salmon in the oven and bake until just cooked through, about 8–10 minutes, depending on the thickness of the fish.

While the fish is in the oven, cook the noodles according to the packet instructions. If you stir them for the first minute, this will help prevent them clumping together (this is particularly helpful with soba or buckwheat noodles, which can really stick together if left to their own devices). Drain, toss in the sesame oil and set aside.

Heat a little oil in a wok or large non-stick frying pan. Add the spring greens, spring onions, garlic, chilli and ginger. Fry until the greens have just wilted, about 3–4 minutes. Toss in the soy sauce, sesame seeds and noodles. Serve the salmon on top of the noodles, with a wedge of lime.

spring or summer green rice rolls

a bit fancy

vegan

MAKES 8, TO SERVE
2-3 AS A MAIN COURSE

100g long-grain brown rice
1 tbsp sunflower
    or light olive oil
1 onion, peeled and
    finely diced
½ tsp dried mint
¼ tsp allspice
8 large spring or summer
    green leaves (a good side-
    plate sized, about 15cm in
    diameter), plus a handful
    of smaller leaves
50g pine nuts, gently
    toasted in a dry frying
    pan until golden
6 pitted dates, chopped
4 tbsp finely chopped parsley
2 tbsp finely chopped
    mint leaves
1 lemon
good olive oil
salt and pepper

Around the eastern Mediterranean there are many versions of stuffed leaves, often using vine leaves, but any good-sized cabbage leaf can be used; try Savoy or January King in winter. These rolls have crunch, sweetness and a fresh herb flavour. The simmering finishes off the rice; as it expands more it plumps up the rolls, and the leaves get extra flavour from the lemony oil coating. If you're short of time though, there's no reason why you can't just boil the leaves, cook the rice fully then roll them up and serve immediately, drizzled with a lemon and olive oil dressing. If the odd roll does split, you can patch it back together. Serve at room temperature as a main course with salads, or on a platter to share as a starter (pictured overleaf).

Rinse the rice in a sieve under cold water. Transfer to a pan, cover with water, add a good pinch of salt and bring to the boil. Cook for 12 minutes.

Heat 1 tablespoon of oil in a small frying pan. Add the onion and fry gently for 10 minutes to soften without colouring. Add the dried mint and allspice to the onion and cook, stirring, for 2 minutes.

Meanwhile, cook the whole green leaves in boiling water for 5 minutes. Drain and refresh under cold water then leave to drain.

Drain the rice and run under cold water to cool it slightly.

Remove the onion from the heat and add the rice, pine nuts, dates, parsley, fresh mint, salt and pepper to season and 1 teaspoon of finely grated lemon zest (about ½ a small lemon).

Lay a green leaf out on your work surface. Chop out the central tough rib in a thin, reverse 'v' shape. Bring one flap of the cut leaf over the other to fill the gap. Spoon a dessertspoon of the rice mixture across the middle of the leaf, leaving a good gap either side. Fold the sides of the leaf in, then roll up to seal it, making a fat cigar/cylinder shape (see overleaf).

Lay the smaller leaves in the bottom of a heavy-bottomed pan, one in which the rolls will fit snugly. Carefully wedge all the rice rolls in, add 200ml of water, the juice from the lemon and a good glug of olive oil. You want to just cover the rolls, so add a splash more water if need be. Put an upturned plate on top, weigh it down (we use a big, clean pebble!), then simmer on the lowest heat possible, no bubbles, or the rolls risk splitting, for 45 minutes. Leave to cool in the pan, then carefully remove them.

VARIATIONS
* Use whole blanched almonds, toasted then chopped, in place of the pine nuts, or try sunflower seeds.
* A little chopped dill adds a different, fresh flavour if you have any, with or instead of the parsley and mint.

spring green and coconut dal

quick & easy

vegan

A colourful and healthy meal. Turmeric and ginger are anti-inflammatory and therefore good for digestion, as is coconut oil, which metabolises well. Organic coconut oil is available to order alongside our veg boxes; it's great for stir-fries and curries, or for roasting veg as it has a slightly different flavour to other oils.

SERVES 2

1 tbsp coconut oil
1 onion, finely sliced
1 large or 2 small garlic
    cloves, finely chopped,
    grated or crushed
4cm piece of fresh ginger,
    peeled and finely grated
1 red chilli, finely sliced
1 tsp black mustard seeds
¼ tsp ground turmeric
1 x 400ml tin coconut milk
100g yellow mung dal lentils,
    rinsed in a sieve
1 tsp coriander seeds,
    toasted and ground
1 tsp cumin seeds, toasted
    and ground
200g spring or summer
    greens, tough ribs
    removed, leaves finely
    shredded
handful of coriander leaves
a squeeze of lime
    or lemon juice
toasted coconut chips
    or toasted desiccated
    coconut, to garnish
salt

Melt the coconut oil in a large pan. Add the onion and fry on a low heat for 10 minutes, stirring occasionally.

Turn up the heat a little and add the garlic, ginger, chilli, mustard seeds and turmeric. Stir for about 1 minute, until you hear the mustard seeds start to pop.

Stir the coconut milk in the can then pour into the pan with the lentils and ground coriander and cumin. Fill the coconut milk can half full with water and add that too. Bring up to the boil, reduce the heat and simmer for about 15 minutes.

Add the greens, stirring in small handfuls at a time, then cook for a further 5–10 minutes, until the lentils are tender and the greens wilted. Keep an eye on the liquid and add more water if needed.

Season the dal with salt, stir in the fresh coriander and add a squeeze of lime or lemon juice to taste. Serve the dal sprinkled with toasted coconut and a few extra coriander leaves.

VARIATIONS
* Use red lentils if you can't find yellow mung dal lentils.
* Use cabbage, spinach or chard instead of the greens.
* Add a 'tarka', a spicy oil, to sprinkle on the top of the dal before serving for an extra kick of spice and chilli: gently heat a tablespoon of coconut oil in a small pan then add 1 teaspoon each of black mustard seeds and cumin seeds, 1 finely sliced large garlic clove and a good pinch of chilli flakes and fry, stirring constantly, for 1–2 minutes until the mustard seeds are popping.

july to october
sweet-
corn

Every gardener loves growing sweetcorn; it is one of the few crops you don't have to bend down to pick and in a hot summer it's easy to grow. But sweetcorn is an import from Mexico, and the Uk is unfortunately on its climatic extremes, so the crop really struggles to ripen in a poor summer. We coax it along with crop covers but it is often not ripe until September when the barbecues are starting to be packed away. In recent years we have been starting the season with sweetcorn from our farm in France.

People make a lot of fuss about eating corn super fresh to get the most sweetness, but modern 'super-sweet' varieties have been bred to delay the conversion of starch to sugar, meaning that they keep pretty well in the fridge for a week, though as with most veg, fresh is always better.

Our favourite cooking method, used at all summer staff parties, is to soak the cobs in water for a few minutes then cook them patiently on a barbecue so they steam inside their husk. When they start to catch they are normally just about done. The husks can be peeled back, making a good handle for eating the cob smothered in butter and/or chilli sauce.

Guy

sweetcorn

storage

Leave sweetcorn cobs wrapped in their protective husks and store in the salad drawer of the fridge. Sweetcorn benefits from being eaten before its natural sugars turn to starch, reducing its sweetness. Ideally, eat it within a day or two but it can be kept for up to a week.

prep

For most recipes, you'll need to remove the husk – just rip off the leaves then pull off the silky threads, or rub them off with a clean tea towel. To cut off the kernels, cut the cob in two through the middle to make two shorter halves. Rest the cut end on the chopping board, and run a sharp knife down each side (a serrated one works best). Try to keep the blade as close to the core as possible so that the kernels come away intact.

The cobs make a good stock for a sweetcorn soup. Place in plenty of water (use about 2 cobs per litre of water) and simmer for at least 20 minutes, or simply as long as it takes you to prepare everything else in the recipe. If you have them, throw in some onion ends and parsley or coriander stalks.

cooking

When your sweetcorn is super-fresh, boiling or steaming are simple and satisfying ways to eat it. Don't skimp on the butter here! But there are plenty of alternative ways of cooking – in the frying pan, the oven and on the barbecue...

boil/steam

Bring a large pan of unsalted water to a boil. Add the cobs and cook until just tender. Alternatively, steam. They'll take 4–10 minutes to either boil or steam, with fresher cobs taking only a few minutes and older ones needing longer. Drain and apply butter and salt. Or cut off the kernels with a knife (see above) and try one of these ideas:

* toss with butter, finely chopped chilli, lime juice, salt, pepper and coriander for a fragrant side dish.

* throw into a salad, e.g. mixed with sliced spring onions, halved cherry tomatoes, crumbled feta, plenty of basil and a vinaigrette. Or with tinned black beans, chopped red pepper, finely diced red onion, lime juice, olive oil and plenty of fresh coriander.

* make fritters: see our recipe on page 70.

grill on the barbecue/roast

Sweetcorn works brilliantly on the barbecue, but if that's not an option, these methods can be adapted for an oven or ridged griddle pan on the stove instead:

TO GRILL INSIDE THE HUSK Soak the whole sweetcorn cobs in a large bowl or bucket of cold water for 20 minutes; this prevents them from burning. Carefully peel back the husks but leave them attached at the stem end. Remove all the straggly silks. If you like, rub the cob with butter or oil and flavourings such as chopped chilli and herbs, then re-cover with the husk. Secure the top with string or a piece of foil if it looks likely to unwrap. Grill over hot coals, turning frequently, until the cob is blackened all over, about 15 minutes. Alternatively, simply place the cobs on the grill as they are and let diners peel away the silks with the husks.

TO GRILL IN FOIL This method is fractionally more effort, but easier to eat afterwards. Remove the husk and silks completely. Rub the cob with butter or oil and flavourings if you wish, then wrap well in foil. Grill over hot coals, turning frequently, until the cob feels soft to the squeeze, about 15 minutes.

TO GRILL NAKED This method gives the most toasty, smoky flavour to the kernels, but it dries them out more than grilling them in their husks or foil. Remove the husk and silks and grill the cobs over hot coals, turning frequently, until the kernels are charred, about 10 minutes. Slather with butter and tuck in. This method also works on a flat cast-iron hotplate.

TO OVEN-ROAST Prepare the cobs in any of the ways listed above – in husks, in foil or naked. Roast in a hot oven (200°C/ Gas 6) for 30–40 minutes, until the kernels have softened. If you've peeled the cobs, put them on a tray and smear them with butter before roasting.

Grilled or roasted corn kernels add a real depth of flavour to recipes. Or make salsa: mix with finely chopped chillies, red onion, tomatoes and garlic, and finish with lime juice and coriander. For a smoother texture (easier for dipping), pulse everything in a processor, or bash in a large mortar. For a toastier flavour, use a cast-iron hot plate to briefly char the whole chillies, tomatoes and garlic cloves (or char them under a hot grill) before chopping them.

sweetcorn

fry/braise

Cut the kernels from the cobs (see page 210) and fry slowly in a generous knob of butter, stirring often. The kernels will part-fry, part-steam in their own moisture. They should be tender after 5–10 minutes (the younger they are, the quicker they'll cook). If they're catching in the pan before they've cooked through, add a dash of water or stock. Alternatively, let them caramelise once they have softened enough to accentuate their sweetness. Season with salt and pepper towards the end of the cooking.

works well with...

* Alliums – garlic, red onions, spring onions
* Bacon
* Beans – black and other shelled beans, green beans
* Butter
* Chilli
* Citrus – lemon and lime juice
* Herbs – especially basil, chervil, coriander, parsley and thyme
* Shellfish
* Squashes, including courgettes
* Tomatoes

IDEAS FOR USING FRIED/ BRAISED SWEETCORN

* Fry chopped onions and a little garlic with the corn. When the onions are soft, add stock (preferably made with the cobs, see page 210) – and other vegetables if you wish (courgettes, butternut squash and black beans are all good) – and simmer into a chunky soup.

* For chowder, fry celery and onions with the corn, stir a spoonful of plain flour into the softened vegetables, then add milk and potatoes and simmer until the potatoes are tender and the liquid has thickened, 20–30 minutes. See our version of corn chowder on page 220.

* Make 'maque choux', a traditional dish from southern Louisiana: braise corn together with onions, garlic, green pepper, celery, tomato and green chilli, adding just a little water or stock to loosen the mix and help it cook. Finish with a dash of soured cream.

* Mix with fried mushrooms and serve alongside roast chicken – a winning combination of flavours.

corn and courgette soup with chilli butter

a bit fancy

vegetarian

freezable

Anna fondly remembers making huge vats of this soup one summer while working at Chez Panisse (the place that inspired Guy to open the Field Kitchen). Creamy and sweet, the trick with this soup is to get a good balance between the corn and courgette flavours. If you don't have time to make the chilli butter, serve it with a squeeze of lime juice and a drizzle of chilli sauce.

SERVES 2 AS A MAIN OR 4 AS A STARTER

4 sweetcorn cobs, husks and silky threads removed

2–3 thyme sprigs

2–3 parsley stalks

1 bay leaf

2 tbsp olive oil

1 medium onion, thinly sliced

2 medium courgettes, evenly sliced

salt and pepper

For the chilli butter

approx. 35g unsalted butter, at room temperature

1 tsp finely chopped parsley leaves

1 tsp finely snipped chives

good pinch of chilli flakes

few drops green Tabasco sauce (if you have it)

½ tsp lime or lemon juice, or to taste

Cut the kernels off the cobs with a knife and set aside. Place the cobs in a large saucepan with 2 litres of water and the herbs to make a corn stock. Bring to a boil then simmer until needed. It will reduce a bit, which is fine.

In a saucepan set over a low heat, heat the oil then slowly fry the onions, adding a pinch of salt, until completely soft but not coloured, about 10 minutes. Add the corn kernels and continue cooking for a further 10 minutes, stirring occasionally. Do not let the onions or corn colour.

Add the courgettes to the pan. Strain the stock and pour enough into the pan with the vegetables just to cover them. Reserve any remaining stock. Add another pinch of salt, bring to a boil, then simmer until the courgettes are tender but still hold their shape, about 10 minutes. Take off the heat and cool for a few minutes.

Meanwhile, make the chilli butter. Mash the butter, parsley, chives, chilli, Tabasco, lime juice and seasoning together with a fork until well mixed and smooth. Store in the fridge until needed.

Purée the soup using a stick blender until totally smooth, then bring to a simmer. Add more stock (or water) if it's too thick. Check the seasoning. Serve garnished with a pat of the chilli butter.

creamed sweetcorn

quick & easy

vegetarian

This serves 3-4 as a simple side dish (it's great with chicken) or 2 as a main course by accompanying it with a bowl of rice or quinoa. Alternatively you can bulk it out with any of the suggestions below.

SERVES 3-4 AS A SIDE

good knob of butter, approx. 25g
1 tbsp sunflower or light olive oil
1 onion, finely diced
kernels from 2 large sweetcorn cobs (see page 208)
4 tbsp double cream
leaves from 3–4 thyme sprigs
½ tsp paprika
salt and pepper

Melt the butter and oil in a saucepan. Add the onion and fry over a low heat for approximately 10 minutes, stirring now and then, until softened.

Add the sweetcorn kernels, cream, thyme and paprika. Season, bring the pan up to a simmer and cook for 10 minutes, stirring now and then to stop it catching, until the corn is tender. Check the seasoning before serving.

VARIATIONS
* Add other things, such as blanched chopped chard or spinach leaves, bacon, garlic, chilli, coriander, cumin, Parmesan.
* For a creamier texture, purée half the mixture once cooked, then stir it back into the pan.
* Fry the corn in coconut oil instead of butter and oil for a slightly different flavour (particularly good if you're adding chilli or Indian spices).

chopped salad with bacon, sweetcorn and avocado

quick & easy

Chopped salads are popular in the **US**, and they're a good way of getting lots of different veg into one meal, while also using up odds and ends. We've kept the dressing light, using yoghurt, lemon and a hint of mustard and garlic. Our mini cucumbers have great flavour, but half a normal cucumber is fine as an alternative.

SERVES 2

300g new or salad potatoes, cut into bite-sized chunks

kernels from 1 sweetcorn cob (see page 210)

150g French beans, topped, tailed and cut into thirds

1 tbsp oil for frying

200g smoked back bacon, diced

½ a crisp lettuce (Cos is good, or use 1 Little Gem), roughly chopped

1 mini cucumber, chopped into bite-sized pieces

1 avocado

salt and pepper

For the dressing

4 tbsp plain yoghurt

1 tsp Dijon mustard

1 garlic clove, finely chopped, grated or crushed

juice of ½ lemon

small bunch of chives, chopped

Boil the potatoes in a large pan of salted water for 8–10 minutes, or until tender. Drain and leave to cool. Boil the corn kernels and French beans in a separate pan of unsalted water for 4 minutes. Drain and leave to cool.

While the veg is cooking, heat the oil in a frying pan. Fry the bacon on quite a high heat, stirring now and then, until crispy, golden and cooked through. Transfer to a large bowl and leave to cool.

Once the veg has cooled, add it to the bowl, with the chopped lettuce and cucumber. Cut the avocado in half and remove the stone. Run a sharp teaspoon inside the skin and scoop out the flesh, then chop into bite-sized pieces and add to the bowl.

In a small bowl, mix together the yoghurt, mustard, garlic, lemon juice and half the chives. Season to taste. Pour the yoghurt dressing over the salad, gently toss together and serve.

vegetable quesadillas

easy

vegetarian (if you use
vegetarian cheese)

SERVES 4

1 small to medium-sized
   butternut squash, peeled
   and cut into 1–2cm dice
1 red pepper, deseeded and
   cut into 1–2cm dice
kernels from 1 sweetcorn
   cob (see page 210)
1 red onion, peeled and
   finely diced
½ tsp ground cumin
¼ tsp ground coriander
¼ tsp paprika
a good pinch of smoked
   paprika
1–2 red chillies (depending
   on heat and your
   preference for it), deseeded
   and finely chopped
light olive oil for roasting,
   frying and brushing
4 large flour tortillas
150g Cheddar, grated
large handful of
   coriander leaves
salt and pepper

Good as a main course, these also make a colourful sharing platter
for a larger gathering. Serve them with a dollop of soured cream
and guacamole.

Heat the oven to 190°C/Gas 5. Toss the squash, pepper, corn,
onion, spices, chilli and 2 tablespoons of olive oil in a large baking
dish. Season with salt and pepper.

Roast the veg in the oven for 35–40 minutes, until tender, tossing
once halfway through so it cooks evenly. Remove from the oven and
turn the temperature down low, to approximately 130°C/Gas 1.

Brush each tortilla on one side with a little oil and put one into
a large non-stick frying pan, oil-side down. Sprinkle some cheese
over one half, then the veg mixture, then a few coriander leaves.

Fold the other half of the tortilla over to make a semi-circle,
gently pressing down with your hands to flatten it slightly. Cook
for a couple of minutes, until the underside of the tortilla is crisp
and golden brown (keep an eye on it so it doesn't burn).

Carefully turn it over and cook the other side until crisp and
golden. Keep warm in the oven while you cook the remainder.
Cut each one in half to serve.

VARIATION
✳ Add some crumbled and fried cooking chorizo or some leftover,
shredded roast chicken for a non-vegetarian version.

sweetcorn, ham hock and watercress chowder

quick & easy

SERVES 4

small knob of butter
splash of olive oil
1 onion, diced
2 celery sticks, diced
1 carrot, diced
grated zest of ½ lemon
1 small potato, diced
kernels from 4 sweetcorn
    cobs (see page 210)
2 garlic cloves, finely
    chopped
leaves from 2 small
    thyme sprigs
1 litre chicken stock
200ml double cream
150g cooked ham hock
    or good-quality baked
    ham, shredded
salt and pepper
bunch of watercress,
    to garnish

Sweetcorn makes a handsome chowder. Here, the salty pork marries well with its sweetness - think Parma ham and melon, or pâté and chutney - and the watercress adds a pepperiness and verdant speckling.

Heat a little butter and olive oil in a large saucepan and cook the onion, celery and carrot over a low heat until starting to soften. Add the lemon zest with the potato, sweetcorn kernels, garlic and thyme and fry for a few minutes. Tip in the stock and simmer for 20 minutes, or until everything is tender.

Stir in the cream and the ham hock and simmer for 2–3 minutes to warm the ham through. Season to taste with salt, pepper and maybe a squeeze of lemon juice. Serve garnished with a good handful of chopped watercress.

VARIATION
* Replace the ham hock with some smoked fish and/or mussels. The fish should cook in the heat of the stock in the last 5 minutes if cut into 2 cm cubes. Use fish stock if you can.

barbecued sweetcorn with burnt lime and sea salt

quick & easy

vegan

SERVES 4

4 sweetcorn cobs with
    the husk still on
2 limes
pinch of brown sugar
butter
flaky or coarse sea salt

A mix of sweet and sour makes an interesting departure from butter and pepper on your corn on the cob. We saw this being done in north India on roadside charcoal burners. If the weather isn't good enough, or you don't have a barbecue, use a cast-iron griddle or heavy-bottomed frying pan and fry the corn in their husks, with no oil. Leave them until the husks cook to a dark brown/black colour, then turn every few minutes so the whole husk is coloured, about 15 minutes in total.

Fire up the barbecue (or see above). Soak the sweetcorn cobs in cold water for 20 minutes.

Throw the cobs on the barbecue and cook for about 15 minutes, turning frequently. The husks will burn but you should be left with perfect smoky corn underneath.

Cut the limes in half, sprinkle the cut side with a little sugar and rub it in with your thumb until dissolved. Press the lime on to the bars of the barbecue until lightly caramelised. Strip the corn from the husk, slather over some butter, squeeze and rub the lime over the corn and sprinkle with salt.

july to october

tomatoes

I reckon we grow some pretty good tomatoes in our tunnels, but only for a brief period and only after rejecting most commercial varieties and even more 'heirloom' ones (not all that is old is worth keeping).

In the UK, without the use of heated glass, tomatoes can be planted in April, start ripening in August and by early October, as sunlight levels dip, are becoming tasteless. Most commercial growers heat their single-glazed glasshouses to enable planting in January when there might be frost outside, and harvesting from March or April. The carbon footprint is insane. Five years ago we took the decision never to buy from heated glass. If you must eat tomatoes after October you will be doing your palate and the planet a favour by buying Italian or Spanish.

The best tomato would be grown south of the Loire, outside in the soil and eaten in the summer. I tried this venture but quickly realised I would go bust in the pursuit of perfection, so ours are all soil-grown under glass or plastic from June to October, and in Spain or Italy from November to June. I reckon they are a reasonable compromise most weeks.

Guy

tomatoes

storage

Do not store tomatoes in the fridge. Chilling damages their flavour compounds. For the best flavour, keep them at room temperature and eat them when they reach peak ripeness – dark red and slightly soft. Don't keep them in an airtight box; the cardboard container or ventilated plastic box they came in is perfect. Eat any bruised or split ones first before they grow mould and spread it to the others.

prep

Tomatoes have a surprisingly resistant skin, so use a super-sharp knife or a small serrated one to chop them. Their flavour is best just after chopping, so prepare tomatoes at the last minute. If you need to prepare them
in advance, avoid adding seasoning or a dressing until later as these will soften the tomatoes and cause water to seep out.

TO GRATE For some dishes, what you need is skinless tomato pulp. Cut the tomato in half along its equator (rather than top to bottom). Swipe the cut side down the large holes of a box grater repeatedly until you are left with just the skin in your hand. The skin is a good addition to the stockpot.

peeling and deseeding

It is rarely necessary to either peel or deseed tomatoes, and in fact both the skin and seeds contribute significantly to the tomato's flavour. However, tomato skins, like those of peppers, can separate and float to the top of a braise or stew, spoiling their appearance, and tomato seeds and the pulp around them are extremely watery, which is why some recipes call for removing them.

TO PEEL Cut a small cross in the base of the tomatoes, just enough to break the skin. Transfer them to a heatproof bowl or use a saucepan. Pour over enough boiling water to cover them. Leave them to soak for about a minute, slightly less if very ripe, then lift them out into a colander and run under the cold tap until cool enough to handle. Peel off the skins, they should come away easily. If not, give them another quick dunk in boiling water.

TO DESEED Cut the tomato in half along its equator. Use a teaspoon to scoop out the sections of seedy pulp, leaving just the flesh behind. (The seeds will enhance the umami flavour of a stock.)

eating tomatoes raw

When tomatoes are at their peak, it's a shame to put them in anything other than a simple sliced tomato salad. A drizzle of extra virgin olive oil and a sprinkle of flaky sea salt is really all you need, though torn basil is a classic addition. For a little variation, try mint or chives instead, and/or walnut oil instead of olive. To accentuate the tomatoes' sweet-and-sour flavour, you could add a tiny sprinkle of sugar and a drizzle of red wine vinegar. For more zing, include a little diced shallot or a few slender rings of red onion. And of course, ragged clouds of creamy mozzarella make an ideal partner.

MORE IDEAS FOR RAW TOMATO

* For an easy tomato salsa, mix diced tomatoes with diced red onion, minced chilli and fresh coriander, adding lime juice, olive oil and salt to taste.

* The classic Middle Eastern tabbouleh salad should be predominantly green from the quantity of parsley used. Mix diced tomatoes with bulghur wheat (pre-soaked in water), chopped spring onions, lemon juice, olive oil, chopped mint and loads of chopped parsley.

* Juicy tomatoes give a second life to torn pieces of stale bread in the Italian salad, panzanella. Mix well, adding basil, a little onion, olive oil and red wine vinegar. Let the salad sit until the juices have rehydrated the bread.

* For 'pa amb tomàquet' (Catalan tomato bread), rub slices of toasted or day-old bread with a cut garlic clove then with half a ripe tomato so that the juices are absorbed. Sprinkle with salt and olive oil.

* For a refreshing cold gazpacho, blend tomatoes with cucumber, red pepper, stale bread (pre-soaked in water), a little red onion and garlic, olive oil and a dash of red wine vinegar to brighten the flavour.

cooking

The key to cooking tomatoes is to cook them for a long time, making them an intense blend of sweet, sour and umami (savoury). Tomatoes can be sliced and baked in gratins along with other vegetables, baked with cheese on pizzas and in tarts (see our galette recipe on page 235), and skinned and gently confited in a bath of olive oil. Our favourite methods are to slowly stew them into a rich sauce or slow-roast them in the oven to concentrate their flavour.

tomatoes

braise/stew

A good tomato sauce is a wonderful resource in the kitchen. You can make it with fresh or tinned tomatoes, or use a combination of the two. Tomato sauce will keep in the fridge for 5 days or the freezer for several months so it's worth making a big batch.

Start by frying a chopped onion, adding some chopped or crushed garlic when it is half-cooked. Or skip the onion and just use garlic. Either way, use plenty of olive oil – it adds flavour – and fry until the onion/garlic is softened and slightly caramelised.

For extra oomph, throw in some anchovies, dried chilli and/or herb sprigs when the onions/garlic are nearly done. Bay, oregano, thyme and basil are particularly good herbs to use.

Add lots of cored, chopped tomatoes and a good pinch of salt, which will help them break down. If you like a more intense flavour, add a dash of red wine and/or a squirt of tomato purée. Start them off over a high heat then reduce to low and simmer for a good hour or two, stirring occasionally. Finish by fishing out the herbs and checking the seasoning. To accentuate the sweet-sour flavour, add a good pinch of sugar and a dash of red wine vinegar.

slow-roast

This is a great option for tomatoes that are too pale and hard to be good raw, and also works well with cherry tomatoes, which will need less time in the oven.

Cut the tomatoes in half horizontally and place them cut-side up in a single layer in a baking dish or roasting tin. Don't crowd the dish or the tomatoes will end up stewing not roasting.

Sprinkle with salt, sugar, pepper and olive oil and add some chopped garlic and thyme leaves, too, if you like. Roast at 160°C/Gas 3 until the tomatoes are shrivelled and caramelised. This will take an hour or two, depending on the water content of the tomatoes (but rest assured: it's hard to over-cook them).

Roast tomatoes make a delicious side dish in their own right, or can be blitzed into a roast tomato passata, and will keep in the fridge for 5 days. Roasted halved cherry tomatoes improve nearly any salad. Try them with boiled green beans and plenty of basil leaves, combined with Puy lentils and crumbled feta, or with chickpeas, fried chorizo and red onion.

tomatoes

IDEAS FOR USING TOMATO SAUCE

As well as eating it on pasta, try:

* Browning meat then pouring over the sauce and braising in the oven until the meat is cooked: meatballs will be done in 30 minutes while beef short ribs will need 2–3 hours to become tender. For a meaty Bolognese-style sauce for pasta, brown minced beef in oil over a high heat then add some red wine and the tomato sauce and simmer for about an hour. Sausage meat works well too: slit open the skins and crumble the meat into the hot oil.

* Spanish and Mexican cooks transform humble white rice by cooking it with plenty of tomato sauce: simply substitute half the cooking water with sauce.

* Fillets and steaks of oily or robust white fish work well. Heat the sauce in a wide pan, perhaps adding capers or olives, then lay in the pieces of fish, which the sauce should nearly cover. Simmer gently until the fish is just cooked through: about 8–10 minutes per 2.5cm thickness of fish.

* Poaching eggs: simmer the sauce in a wide pan until thickened. Make depressions in the sauce and crack an egg into each. Season the eggs with salt, cover the pan and simmer for 6–10 minutes over a low heat until the eggs are cooked to your liking.

* 'Baked beans': combine fried onions and garlic, tomato sauce and tinned beans (haricot are classic, but any will do, or even chickpeas) in a heavy-bottomed saucepan. You can add fried bacon, brown sugar or molasses, vinegar and spices such as mustard powder, cloves and chilli. Simmer on the stove for an hour or two until reduced and thickened, stirring occasionally.

* For a ratatouille-style dish, fry a chopped onion in 2 tablespoons of olive oil for 10 minutes, stirring now and then. Once the onion is softened, add some sliced garlic. Cook for a further 2 minutes then add a diced aubergine and stir for 5 minutes. Add 2 diced peppers and 2 diced courgettes and cook, stirring for 2 minutes. Pour in enough passata or chopped tomatoes (tinned or fresh) to cover, season and simmer for about 15 minutes or so, until the veg is tender. Finish with fresh basil.

quick-fry

Although tomatoes usually suit long, slow cooking, quickly fried cherry tomatoes make a delicious and easy pasta sauce that can be on plates in minutes.

While the pasta is cooking, heat olive oil in a wide saucepan. Fry finely chopped garlic over medium heat for a couple of minutes until just starting to colour, then increase the heat to high and throw in halved cherry tomatoes, a pinch of salt and some chilli flakes if you like. Fry vigorously, tossing the tomatoes around the pan. After a couple of minutes, they should be softening and starting to colour, but still holding their shape. Add the drained pasta to the pan, along with a little of its cooking water and another drizzle of olive oil. Toss everything together until a sauce begins to emulsify around the pasta. Finish with pepper, basil and torn mozzarella. Toss once more and serve immediately.

work well with...

* Aubergine
* Bacon
* Cheese – especially feta, Gruyère, mozzarella
* Eggs
* Garlic
* Herbs – especially basil, coriander, mint oregano, tarragon, thyme
* Meat – beef, chicken, lamb, pork
* Olives and olive oil
* Salt
* Spices – anise, chilli, cinnamon, clove

OVEN-DRIED TOMATOES

Since in England you'll sadly never be able to rely on the sun, try this method: halve and deseed the tomatoes (see page 224). Season with salt and place cut-side down on a rack inside a roasting tin. Place in a very low oven (max 100°C / Gas ¼) with the door wedged open a crack with a skewer to prevent heat and condensation building up. After 6–8 hours the tomatoes should be dried but still fleshy. Turn them over halfway through. If you sprinkle them with vinegar then cover them with olive oil, oven-dried tomatoes will keep in a sterilised jar in the fridge for many weeks.

tomato and tarragon salad with tapenade toast

quick & easy

Tapenade is a French olive paste and can be eaten as a dip or spread. This recipe is great for sharing as a starter or light lunch. It will make more tapenade than you'll need for one meal, but it's not worth making less, and it keeps well for a few days in the fridge. You could use shop-bought tapenade if you prefer, although making your own is easy and satisfying.

SERVES 4

For the tapenade toast
200g pitted black olives
2 tbsp capers (if in brine, soak in water for 20 minutes then drain)
3 preserved anchovies
1 large or 2 small garlic cloves, finely chopped
leaves from 3 thyme sprigs
1 tbsp chopped parsley leaves, plus a little extra for garnishing
juice of ½ lemon, more to taste
approx. 5 tbsp olive oil
slices of ciabatta or sourdough, griddled or toasted

For the tomato salad
8 large tomatoes (a few more if smaller)
2 pinches of caster sugar
4 tbsp olive oil
juice from ¼ of a lemon, more to taste
1 good tsp Dijon mustard
3 tbsp tarragon leaves, roughly chopped
salt and black pepper

Make the tapenade by blitzing the olives, capers, anchovies, garlic and thyme in a food processor, then adding the parsley, lemon juice and just enough oil to make a rough paste. (If you don't have a food processor, pound the ingredients in a pestle and mortar, then stir in the lemon juice and oil.) Season to taste: you'll need little or no salt, as the mixture is already salty from the anchovies.

Thinly slice the tomatoes and arrange on a platter. Sprinkle with the sugar.

Whisk the remaining olive oil, lemon juice and mustard together. Taste and add more lemon juice or oil if needed. Pour over the tomatoes. Sprinkle with salt and pepper and scatter over the tarragon.

Spread the tapenade on to the ciabatta and sprinkle over a little extra parsley. Serve with the tomato salad.

shakshuka

quick & easy

vegetarian (if you use
vegetarian cheese)

This is a North African dish with spiced peppers, tomatoes and eggs. There are many variations across the globe, such as 'huevos rancheros' in Mexico, which is served with tortillas and avocado. It makes a good dinner or Sunday brunch, especially with warm pitta to soak up the juices. Instead of feta you could try Wootton White, an organic British feta-style cheese.

SERVES 2

2 tbsp sunflower
   or light olive oil
1 large or 2 smaller onions,
   finely sliced
2 red peppers, deseeded
   and thinly sliced or diced
1 large or 2 smaller garlic
   cloves, finely chopped,
   crushed or grated
1 red chilli, deseeded
   and finely chopped
1 tsp ground cumin
1 tsp paprika
¼ tsp smoked paprika
¼ tsp ground turmeric
500g tomatoes, skinned
   (see page 222) and diced
1 bay leaf
4 eggs
75g feta (½ a standard pack)
handful of parsley, chopped
handful of coriander,
   chopped
salt and pepper
warm pitta bread, to serve
   (optional)

Heat the oil in a non-stick frying pan. Add the onions and peppers. Cook on a low heat for about 10 minutes, until the onions are translucent and the peppers have started to soften. Add the garlic, chilli, cumin, both paprikas and turmeric and stir for 2 minutes.

Add the tomatoes and bay leaf. Season with salt and pepper and simmer for about 20 minutes, until the mixture has thickened to a sauce (the timing will depend on the width of your pan). If it looks like drying out too much, add a little water.

Use a spoon to make 4 hollows in the sauce and break an egg into each. Cook on a low heat for 5–10 minutes or until the eggs are set to the consistency you like. Divide the eggs and sauce between two bowls, taking care not to break the eggs. Crumble over the feta, sprinkle over the herbs and serve with the pitta, if you like.

devilled tomatoes

quick & easy

vegetarian

SERVES 2

6 ripe tomatoes
olive oil

For the devilling sauce
1 tsp soft light brown sugar
1 tsp paprika
1 tsp English mustard
  powder
½ tsp cayenne pepper
1 tsp Worcestershire sauce
1 tbsp red wine vinegar
pinch of salt

To devil something is a very English way of saying 'add spice and heat': if the end product doesn't make your nose sweat then you're not doing it right! This devilling sauce works well with many different kinds of grilled or fried meat and fish. Try spooning it over a whole mackerel before grilling, or marinating a chicken breast in it overnight then pan-frying. It keeps well in the fridge for a few days, so experiment at your leisure.

Heat the oven to 200°C/Gas 6. Cut the tomatoes in half horizontally, rub lightly with olive oil and place in a roasting tin, cut-side up.

Mix all the devilling ingredients together. Spoon the sauce over the tomatoes and roast in the oven for 15–20 minutes until cooked through and starting to colour. Check halfway and spoon any sauce that has collected in the bottom of the tin back over the tomatoes.

tomato and Gruyère galette

quick & easy

vegetarian

A galette is a free-form tart that doesn't need a tin. Its irregular shape is its rustic charm so don't aim for perfection here. This works just as well with shop-bought puff pastry; for the best flavour, go for an all-butter version. Eat warm or at room temperature, with a green salad on the side.

SERVES 4

300g all-butter puff pastry
1 egg, beaten with a pinch of salt
2–3 tsp Dijon mustard
a generous handful of grated Gruyère cheese (or use a strong farmhouse Cheddar)
handful of oregano or basil leaves, roughly chopped or torn
1 heaped tsp fresh thyme leaves
3 or 4 full-flavoured tomatoes, depending on their size, cored and sliced
extra virgin olive oil
salt and pepper

Lightly flour your work surface and rolling pin and roll the pastry into a rough circle or square, 2–3mm thick. Trim the edges and lay it on a baking sheet lined with parchment. Brush all over with a thin layer of beaten egg (retaining the remaining egg for later). Spread a thin layer of mustard over the top, stopping short of the edge by about 4cm.

Sprinkle the cheese over the mustard, then add the herbs. Lay over tomato slices, slightly overlapping, then drizzle with a little olive oil and season with salt and pepper.

Fold the edges over the filling to form a border – there should still be plenty of tomatoes visible. Leave the folds loose rather than squishing them down as this will help the pastry bake through in the oven. Chill the galette in the fridge for 20 minutes before you bake it. Heat the oven to 190°C/Gas 5, putting a rack near the bottom.

Brush the rest of the egg over the pastry border and bake for around 40 minutes or until the pastry is cooked through and starting to brown. Undercooked pastry is horrible, so make sure you cook it long enough. If the tomatoes look in danger of burning, cover them with a piece of foil or baking parchment.

Let cool for a few minutes then slide on to a board or serving plate.

tomato and courgette pasta bowl

quick & easy

vegetarian (if you
use veg stock and
vegetarian cheese)

SERVES 4

sunflower or light olive oil,
    for frying
1 onion, finely chopped
2 garlic cloves, finely
    chopped
1 tbsp tomato purée
5–6 tomatoes, depending on
    size, skinned (see page 224)
    and diced
2 courgettes, cut into
    2cm dice
2 carrots, cut into 2cm dice
1 litre chicken or good
    veg stock
200g small pasta shapes
    e.g. orzo, small conchiglie
    or macaroni
handful of basil leaves
50g Parmesan or vegetarian
    alternative, grated
extra virgin olive oil,
    for drizzling

This is a light, one-pot dinner, where the taste of simply cooked vegetables shines through. If you can't find small pasta shapes, break spaghetti into small lengths.

Heat 3 tablespoons of oil in a large saucepan. Add the onion and fry very gently, stirring now and then to stop it catching, for 10 minutes. Add the garlic and stir for 2 minutes.

Add the tomato purée, tomatoes, courgettes and carrots and stir for 2 minutes. Add the stock and season with salt and pepper. Bring to the boil. Add the pasta, reduce the heat and simmer for about 10 minutes, until the pasta is just tender.

Shred the basil leaves and stir them into the sauce, with half the Parmesan. Check the seasoning and serve drizzled with a little extra virgin olive oil and sprinkled with the rest of the cheese.

VARIATION
Swap the wheat pasta for some rice pasta or cooked beans, such as cannellini, to make a gluten-free version.

occasional
visitors to
the box

The veg in this section all have a short season or a small yield. They may appear occasionally in your veg box (usually with some cooking suggestions), or on our extras list for you to add to your order.

Guy

borlotti beans

From the kidney bean family, borlotti are plump, creamy and substantial – pinkish-brown in colour, with red streaks. The only downside is they lose these pretty speckled markings when cooked.

When I occasionally encountered borlotti beans in London farmers' markets before we grew them, I was outraged by their price but bowled over by their flavour. Begrudgingly I accepted that foodies can be right and became determined to grow them myself.

Believing our climate borderline appropriate for the crop at best, I tried twice on our farm in France, only to be defeated by birds and bean seed fly. However, some of our co-op farms in Devon have been more successful and we're able to send them out in the boxes from time to time – the yield is just not big enough to send them out every week.

They are best hand-picked when they are half-dried on the plant ('demi-sec') which means the beans will continue to ripen. You need to wait until the pods have got their mottled pink colour; picking the pods when they are green outside means the beans inside aren't ready to eat. Picking is slow and supplies limited, which is why they are an 'occasional visitor' or an 'extra' in the boxes. When fully dry they can be machine harvested at a fraction of the cost, but they never taste as good.

storage

Keep borlotti fresh by storing them in their pods in the fridge in the bag they came in. They should last at least a week, then may begin to mould. To keep them longer you can spread the pods out on a rack in a warm, airy room and let them dry out. Pop out the beans and store them at room temperature. If properly dried they will stay good for a year.

prep and cooking

Open up the pods with your fingers and pop out the beans – a satisfying job, especially if you can find a companion to help you. There's no need to wash the beans. Add the pods to the compost. Borlotti beans are best cooked on the stove with a little water and aromatics, such as bay leaves, onions, garlic and other hardy herbs (see our recipe opposite). The cooked beans will last in the fridge for 5 days and can be used in numerous ways – the list of suggestions opposite is just a starting point.

braised borlotti beans

quick & easy

vegan

SERVES 4

about 500g shelled 'demi-sec' borlotti beans
a carrot, onion and celery stick, if available,
    peeled if needed and halved
a few garlic cloves, peeled
a dried or fresh chilli (optional)
parsley stalks, bay leaves, thyme sprigs
    (if available)
olive oil
salt

Place beans in a pot and cover with cold
water by an inch. Add the aromatics you
have to hand, a good glug of olive oil and
a generous pinch of salt.

Bring to a boil then reduce the heat and
simmer gently, partially covered, until the
beans are tender. Add more water as needed
to keep the beans just covered, but try not to
stir as the beans may break up. They will take
around 30–40 minutes to cook, depending on
their freshness. Test several beans to be sure:
they should have lost all hints of chalkiness.

Fish out the vegetables and herbs and check
the seasoning. Drain and eat immediately,
drizzled with the best olive oil you have,
or store in the fridge with enough of the
cooking liquor to cover and use as below.

IDEAS FOR USING BRAISED BORLOTTI BEANS

* A hearty stew, with added vegetables
or meat. Chorizo and other pork
products work especially well. Wilt
spinach straight into the stew just
before serving.

* A cold bean salad, with fresh
red onion, parsley and vinaigrette.
Tinned tuna is a good addition.

* A side dish for a big roast or braise,
perhaps with extra fried onions and
garlic muddled through, and plenty
of fresh herbs. This is particularly
good with lamb and pork.

* Puréed and spread on toast, with
a good drizzle of olive oil. Fried
sage leaves are great on top of this.

* Puréed with extra garlic, tahini,
chilli and lemon juice for an
alternative to hummus.

* Mixed into pasta and served hot
with grated Parmesan, a drizzle of
olive oil and plenty of black pepper.

edamame beans

For several years these immature soya beans have been dubbed a 'superfood' and are the snack of choice for urban, barfly hipsters while they wait for their sushi and discuss their omega 3 to 6 balance. Who knows what inspired John Walter Symons, a cider-making veg grower and one of our founder co-op members, to sow a field of edamame on his Devon farm, but the first we heard of this was when a few bean-laden plants appeared on my desk. Always up for a challenge, I spent the evening researching and cooking, and they got a firm thumbs up from all. They are best lightly boiled, salted and eaten out of their pods as a snack; no-one will get me claiming superfood status for anything, but edamame must be better for you than a pork scratching.

cooking

Boil or steam the whole pods for 5 minutes. Drain, refresh in a bowl of ice-cold water, then pod and sprinkle with a little sea salt. The quickest way to pod, rather than splitting the edge of the pod open like broad beans, is to lightly press your thumb and first fingertips against the flatter edge of the pod. The beans will fly out, so keep the pods inside the bowl.

Alternatively, toss the whole pods in a baking dish in just enough olive oil to coat, season and roast at 180°C/Gas 4 for approximately 15 minutes, until just tender. Edamame beans are a mainstay of Asian salads – try tossing cooked rice noodles with a little sesame oil, then mixing cooked and podded edamame beans with shredded carrot, sliced peppers and a soy, chilli and garlic dressing.

edamame, rocket and mozzarella salad

quick & easy   vegetarian (if you use vegetarian cheese)

Simple combinations of ingredients bring out edamame's delicate flavour: here creamy mozzarella, peppery leaves and lemon and olive oil dressing. This will serve 2 as a starter or light lunch - add some crusty bread for a more substantial dish.

SERVES 2

200g edamame beans, in their pods
½ tsp Dijon mustard
1 tbsp lemon juice (about ½ a small lemon)
3 tbsp olive oil
50g rocket leaves (or use some peppery
    salad leaves or watercress)
125g mozzarella (or try a little crumbled
    sheep's cheese)
salt and pepper

Boil the edamame beans in a pan of salted boiling water for 5 minutes. Drain, refresh in a bowl of ice-cold water, then drain again. Pod the beans.

Whisk the mustard, lemon juice and olive oil together in a small bowl. Season with salt and pepper. Taste and add more seasoning, mustard or lemon juice if needed. Gently toss the leaves and beans in just enough of the dressing to coat (you may not need all of it). Tear up the mozzarella and tuck it into the salad. Alternatively, crumble other cheeses over the top.

tomatillos

I have found my dream crop; now all I have to do is persuade you to eat it. Most commercial fruit and veg varieties have been bred over many generations for uniformity, yield, earliness and cosmetic appearance. In the process they have lost the ability to look after themselves, needing to be mollycoddled with irrigation and constant weeding and, for non-organic farmers, agrochemicals and fertilisers to coax out their impressive yields. To make matters worse, in our search for culinary stimulation we have often taken crops outside their climatic comfort zones. In contrast to this battle, it is such a joy to grow a crop where it is really happy, as we find with the tomatillo harvest on our farm in France. Even in dreadful growing years, when their distant American cousins the chillies and peppers struggle, the tomatillos are rampant.

Tomatillos hail from Central and South America and are like a green unripe tomato. Tangy, with a citrus sweetness, I grill, barbecue and roast them and have even included them in stews, but there is no doubt that their best use is in a Mexican salsa verde (see our recipe on page 245) where they combine so well with coriander, garlic, and chilli.

storage

Tomatillos should be eaten when they are firm and green. Store them in the salad drawer of your fridge and use them within a week.

prep

You will need to remove the inedible papery husk and wash off the sticky sap that sometimes coats the fruits. Most recipes call for tomatillos to be cooked – this reduces their acidity and brings out their sweetness while retaining their wonderfully fresh taste.

cooking

Boiling is the quickest way to cook them. Simply place them in a saucepan, cover with cold water, bring to a boil and simmer for 5–7 minutes until soft. Drain and let cool. You can also chop or purée tomatillos and add them to a stew for the last 30–45 minutes of cooking.

Or they can be left whole and roasted with a little oil and salt. Spread them over a roasting tin in a single layer and cook in a very hot oven (around 220°C/Gas 8) until softened and browned in places, about 20 minutes. Check on them halfway through and stir so that they caramelise evenly. They will lose their bright green colour and become soft and juicy.

tomatillo salsa verde

quick & easy

vegan

This is a classic Mexican way to serve tomatillos. You can use cooked tomatillos if you want a sweeter condiment (boil for 5-7 minutes before following the recipe), but kept raw they have a sour freshness that's perfect for a summer's day. This lends itself to all things grilled – chicken, pork and white fish. Pile on to tortilla chips or into soft wraps along with pork or chicken.

SERVES 4

1 small red onion, finely diced
1 teaspoon brown sugar
zest and juice of 1 lime
400g tomatillos, husks removed and rinsed well
1–2 chillies (depending on heat preference)
1 small garlic clove
20g coriander
sea salt

Mix the onion with the sugar and juice and zest of the lime and leave to sit in a shallow bowl for 30 minutes – the acid from the lime takes away the raw edge of the onions. Meanwhile, pulse the tomatillos and chilli in a food processor with a dash of water until roughly chopped (or do it by hand). Finely mince the garlic into a paste with a pinch of salt and roughly chop the coriander. Mix all the ingredients together and season well with a little more salt, tasting as you go and adding more lime or sugar if needed.

SOLIDIFIED SALSA

If left, a tomatillo salsa may solidify into a jelly-like mass. This is normal and harmless: tomatillos contain pectin that reacts with acid to form a gel. Just give it a stir and maybe add a dash of water to loosen it further.

wild garlic

Wild garlic, or ransoms, is one of the joys of the spring. Its short season comes when other fresh leaves are in short supply and, better still, it comes free to those with the time and knowledge to forage for it. For many years my children and their friends have paid for their summer holidays in a busy few weeks picking in the woods. Such is its popularity with our customers that each year I am gathering and spreading the seeds in newly planted woodland. My favourite use of ransoms is to fold the leaves into an omelette. It is also good raw in salads, wilted over pasta or added to soups, curries and stews at the end.

storage

We send wild garlic out in plastic bags. Keep them in your fridge, and use quickly, before the leaves wilt.

prep

Wash wild garlic well before use, pick off any large stalks, then use whole leaves or shred them.

cooking

Wild garlic wilts and cooks quickly. Whether you use whole or shredded leaves, they cook in just a minute or two.

CALLING ALL GARLIC LOVERS

There's no need to choose! For the ultimate garlic hit combine regular, wet and wild garlic in a pasta dish, risotto or dip.

potato and wild garlic soup

quick & easy

vegetarian (if using veg stock)

freezable

We send you out wild garlic leaves but not the flowers, as they're too delicate to travel. The flowers are very pretty in soups and on salads, so collect a handful if you pass them when they're out in April and May. This is good served with rye bread or thickly buttered cheese scones. Increase the amount of wild garlic if you dare!

SERVES 4

2 tbsp sunflower or light olive oil
1 large onion, finely diced
600g potatoes, peeled and diced
1.2 litres chicken or vegetable stock
50g wild garlic leaves, shredded,
   plus a few extra to serve
crème fraîche or double cream, to serve
wild garlic flowers (optional)

Heat the oil in a large saucepan. Add the onion and fry on a low heat for 10 minutes, stirring often, until softened without colouring. Add the potatoes and stock. Bring to the boil, reduce the heat and simmer for 20 minutes, or until the potatoes are tender.

Add the wild garlic leaves, reserving a few shreds for garnishing the soup. Blend until smooth. Reheat in the pan, seasoning to taste. Serve with a swirl of crème fraîche or double cream, a few shreds of wild garlic and some wild garlic flowers if you have them.

wild garlic butter

quick & easy   vegetarian   freezable

This goes with all sorts of veg: toss it with roasted broccoli, melt it into wilted spring greens or warm carrots, or lay a slice on top of fried mushrooms on toast. It's also good with meat. Try a slice on top of a steak or stuffed between the skin and breast of a chicken before roasting.

MAKES 250G

250g butter, left to soften at room temperature
good handful of wild garlic leaves (approx. 25g),
   very finely chopped
juice of ½ a lemon

Beat the chopped wild garlic leaves and lemon juice into the butter. Arrange in a rough sausage shape in the middle of some cling film. Roll the cling film tightly around the butter and twist it securely at both ends. Keep in the fridge for a few days or the freezer for longer, slicing bits off as you need them.

wet garlic

Cultivated garlic is grown from cloves planted 2cm under well-drained soil from November to March. By May a strong leek-like plant should have developed, with the swollen base starting to differentiate into what, given another month would be a new bulb of eight to fifteen cloves. If pulled in this immature 'wet' state, the whole plant, leaves and all, can be used without any peeling - it is much milder and sweeter than mature garlic. Think of it as garlicky spring onion and add it to salads and salsas, or use it generously in your cooking; it is particularly good in stir-fries. Unlike dried garlic, wet garlic is best added towards the end of cooking as you only need it to wilt down, like other greens. The aim is to keep as much of the fresh green colour and flavour as possible.

storage

Unlike dried garlic, wet garlic needs to be kept in the fridge. It'll stay fresh for a week or two in the salad drawer. After that you may need to relegate its outer layers and stalk to the compost or a garlicky stock.

prep

Really fresh, immature garlic bulbs can be eaten in their entirety, stem and all. Only peel it if the outer layer seems dry: then just remove the roots, cut the bulb and stem in half lengthways so that each half can rest flat, and slice them crossways as thinly as you can, using the stalk as well as the bulb.

cooking

Where you might have used a couple of cloves of mature garlic for a dish you can use a whole stick of wet garlic – don't hold back. Whether fried, roasted or boiled it needs a little less time to cook than regular garlic. We haven't given you a specific recipe as shredded it can be substituted for dried garlic in any recipe; its milder flavour means you can use a good handful or two. If you don't want to use it all immediately, shredded wet garlic will freeze in a tub and can be taken out and thrown straight into dishes as you need it.

fresh herbs

Fresh herbs can transform a dish by adding depth or brightness to the flavour, as well as adding interest to the overall look.

basil

Basil is a delicate herb that bruises easily so treat it with care. Spicy and fresh in equal measure, basil pairs beautifully with tomatoes – raw, roasted or cooked into a sauce. To avoid it going black, store it somewhere cool rather than cold and slice the leaves with a very sharp knife, or tear them with your hands. Whizzed into a pesto (see pages 44 and 182), basil will keep its vibrant colour and flavour for a couple of days in the fridge if covered with a layer of oil. To store pesto for longer, freeze it in little tubs. Once you've picked off the leaves, keep the stalks and throw them into a bubbling tomato sauce to infuse, then fish them out before serving.

chervil

The flavour of chervil is somewhere between mild parsley and tarragon, with a note of aniseed. It pairs well with delicate flavours such as poultry, fish, eggs and summer vegetables. Use chervil as a garnish, or blitz with tarragon, chives, parsley, oil and capers to make a vibrant green sauce that is fantastic on salmon.

chives

Chives have a mild oniony flavour that makes them very useful in the kitchen. Pair them with eggs, potatoes, cheese, fish or anything else that usually benefits from a dose of onion or garlic. Chop them finely to release their flavour and add them at the end of cooking, or use them in salads or as a garnish. Mixed into sour cream, chives make a lively dip for potato wedges. The purple flowers are edible, too: break them up and sprinkle them over a potato salad.

coriander

Grassy, cooling and citrussy, coriander leaf is a match for hot and spicy food – Indian, Thai, Vietnamese and Mexican. Try it, too, on tomato salads, in guacamole or with fatty meats such as lamb and pork. Coriander's flavour dies when cooked, so use it raw as a garnish or add it to a dish right at the end of cooking. Coriander stalks can be whizzed, along with garlic, ginger or galangal, green chilli and shallots, into a vibrant green Thai curry paste (see page 257).

dill

Feathery dill's mild aniseed flavour is underrated in the UK. Try it in salads such as tomato, cucumber and radish, or with beetroot and feta. Dill also pairs brilliantly with sour dairy produce – soured cream, yoghurt and cream cheese – and enhances simply cooked salmon, chicken, new potatoes and eggs.

mint

Mint has a fresh, sweet flavour and cooling aftertaste. It works well with fatty foods such as lamb or spicy Middle-Eastern dishes. It is particularly good with feta, yoghurt, cucumber, melon, peas, oranges and aubergine. Mint is also great in drinks, from a soothing mint tea to a refreshing mojito. Mint leaves bruise easily: a good way to cut them, which avoids this, is to stack a few in a neat pile, roll up tightly like a cigar and then slice crossways into thin ribbons.

oregano and marjoram

These herbs are closely related and can be used interchangeably. Quite strongly flavoured, especially when dried, oregano and marjoram can stand up to spicy flavours, for example in a Mexican-style beef or bean chilli. They work well with meat, fish and vegetables to be grilled or roasted, along with some garlic and olive oil. They also enhance tomato sauces for pasta and pizza, especially with a little red chilli in the mix. As strong herbs, they are generally not used as a garnish and are better off added early, to give them time to cook and infuse.

parsley (flat-leaf or curly)

Fresh, cool and green, parsley's powerful flavour is versatile, be it in flat-leaf or curly form. Stronger flavoured flat-leaf is perhaps more favoured, but unless you particularly want the flat leaves for decoration, they're pretty interchangeable in recipes. Just use a little more curly for the same flavour.

sorrel

Common sorrel has arrow-shaped leaves, which look a little like miniature dock leaves. Its flavour is strongly acidic and sour. Combine young sorrel with other leaves for a zingy green salad, but go easy on the vinegar in the dressing. Use it to brighten up buttery mashed potatoes, meat or cheese pies, or rich spicy stews as is done in parts of West Africa.

tarragon

A little tarragon goes a long way so use its distinctive anise flavour with care. It goes well with fish, chicken and egg dishes. It suits certain vegetables too, especially asparagus, mushrooms and carrots. Try it in a simple mushroom omelette or an asparagus quiche. Tarragon excels in creamy sauces for chicken and rabbit, and in Béarnaise sauce for steak. Cut tarragon quickly blackens, so chop it at the last minute. Tarragon vinegar is delicious in chicken salads: infuse a few sprigs in a bottle of white wine vinegar or cider vinegar for a week or so.

STORING HERBS

To lengthen the life of fresh herbs, remove any rubber bands or ties and swish the herbs around in a big bowl of cold water. Let them sit for a few minutes while any dirt sinks to the bottom. Lift out then spin dry in a salad-spinner or by shaking in a clean tea towel. Layer the herbs in a plastic box with sheets of kitchen paper to absorb the remaining water. Finish with a final sheet of paper, then seal and store in the fridge. Many herbs will keep like this for a week or even two.

Basil

Coriander

Bay

Dill

Chives

Chervil

Mint

Sage

Thyme

Rosemary

Parsley (flat leaf)

Parsley (curly)

Oregano
(marjoram looks very similar)

Tarragon

salad leaves

A really good green salad can be a revelation: packed with flavour, texture and colour – from fiery mustard leaves to earthy rainbow baby chard, crunchy pak choi and pretty beetroot leaves (which do indeed taste of beetroot). Give your leaves a wash, spin them dry, dress simply and relish the different flavours.

MILD LEAVES

ashbrook lettuce

Mild and crunchy. Similar to baby leaf lettuce, Ashbrook adds balance to peppery companions in your salad mix.

chard

Earthy and mild, yet tender to munch on. Mixed baby chard leaves add colour with red, yellow and green leaves.

mizuna kyoto

The green cousin of mizuna red baron, crunchy and flavourful.

mizuna red baron

This colourful leaf is a deep dark red. Mild in flavour with a crunch.

pak choi Hanakan

Refreshing and crunchy. This is the baby leaf of the pak choi widely used in stir-fries. Makes a crunchy and sweet addition to your salad pack.

red titan beetroot leaf

Strikingly dark and great to crunch on, this leaf tastes a little like beetroot.

tatsoi

Similar in taste to its cousin, pak choi, but with a rounder leaf.

PEPPERY LEAVES – HOT/MUSTARDY

golden streaks mustard

Like its ruby streaks cousin, this bright green variety adds colour and a hot, mustardy flavour.

komatsuna

Looks a little like spinach with a bit of a crunch. Mild mustardy flavour.

red zest mustard

Peppery, with a crunchy and bitter twist at the end. Adds a little heat to your salad.

ruby streaks mustard

Full flavoured. Mustardy and hot, with a peppery finish.

sky rocket

Expect the usual peppery flavour as you crunch on this leaf, a variety of more common rocket.

watercress

Peppery and refreshing, watercress is great in mixed salads or served solo alongside roast beef.

STORING LEAVES

Gently swish the leaves around in a big bowl of cold water. Let them sit for a couple of minutes so that any dirt sinks to the bottom of the bowl. Lift them out with your hands then spin them dry in a salad-spinner or by shaking them in a clean tea towel. If not using straight away, place them in a plastic box lined with sheets of kitchen paper to absorb the remaining water. Finish with a final sheet of paper, then seal and store in the fridge. Stored like this salad leaves can keep for up to a week.

Mizuna Kyoto

Pak choi Hanakan

Ruby streaks mustard

Red titan beetroot leaf

Golden streaks mustard

Sky rocket

Mizuna red baron

Ashbrook lettuce

Komatsuna

chillies

In general small chillies are super-hot and big fat ones are mild, but there are exceptions to this rule, and in any case heat varies from plant to plant. So avoid unwelcome surprises by tasting a little from the tip before adding a whole load of chilli to your dish. Most green chillies will ripen into red chillies given time. They tend to taste fresher, like a green pepper, while red chillies tend to be warmer, sweeter and fruitier. In most recipes the two are interchangeable. Store chillies in a plastic bag in the fridge and use within a couple of weeks. Or dry them – see TIP below.

VARIETIES *IN ORDER OF HEAT*

cherry bomb
The roundest, earliest, thickest-skinned and mildest – great for inclusion in a salsa, stir-fry or even a salad.

fresno
Slightly more elongated and a bit hotter.

cayenne
Hot but by no means extreme. Well-suited to a chilli con carne. Because it has a thinner skin, it is also good for home drying – see TIP opposite.

Scotch bonnet
Extremely hot! Handle with care and use in moderation. Scotch Bonnets have a distinctive flavour that's used a lot in Caribbean and West African cuisines.

IDEAS FOR CHILLI LOVERS

Blitz the ingredients for these classic chilli pastes in a food processor. Both will keep in the fridge for a few days, or freeze in small tubs or ice-cube trays.

* Thai green curry paste: The essential base for a fish, chicken or vegetable curry, made with 5 green chillies, 2 tbsp roughly chopped garlic, 2 tbsp chopped lemongrass, 4 peeled and chopped shallots, 1 tbsp grated fresh ginger, 1 tbsp chopped kaffir lime leaves, 2 tsp toasted and ground coriander, 2 tsp toasted and ground cumin seeds, 1 tbsp soy sauce, 2 tbsp sunflower oil, a little pepper.

* Chermoula: An Arabic paste usually used to flavour fish and seafood dishes, made with 4 chopped red chillies, the juice of 2 lemons, 2 chopped garlic cloves, 1 tbsp toasted and ground cumin seeds, ½ tbsp toasted and ground coriander seeds, 1 tbsp paprika, pinch of saffron, 100ml olive oil, small handful fresh coriander leaves, salt and pepper. Toss it with root vegetables before roasting, or use as a marinade for fish, lamb or chicken.

TIP: DIY CHILLI POWDER

To dry chillies, leave them somewhere warm, or thread a needle and cotton through the stalks and hang them up; they'll be dry in a few days. You can use them whole or grind them into a powder: remove their stems, then break them open and take out the seeds. Break the flesh into pieces and grind in a spice grinder or with a pestle and mortar. Store in a jar, preferably somewhere dark to stop the colour fading.

basic recipes

vegetable stock

Use what you have! It could be the guts of a butternut squash with a couple of onion ends to make a quick squash stock for a squash risotto, or it could be a medley of odds and sods collected over the week. Here are a few tips:

* Leave out potatoes and brassicas, i.e. the stinky cabbage family.

* Try to keep a plastic box going in the fridge to collect veg scraps.

* If you have them, throw in an extra carrot, onion, leek and celery stick, peeled as needed and roughly chopped.

* Herbs are good too, especially parsley, thyme and bay, but avoid strong herbs such as rosemary and sage.

* Herb stalks are ideal, so next time a recipe calls for parsley leaves, keep the stalks in a bag in the fridge: they will last for a week or two.

* A few peppercorns will add a subtle peppery note, but avoid salt as you can add it later when using your stock.

* A squirt of tomato purée (or a spare tomato), chopped mushroom stalks and a Parmesan rind will all add a helpful umami (savoury) dimension. Parmesan rinds wrapped in cling film will keep in the fridge for weeks.

Place everything in a large saucepan and cover with cold water.

Bring to a boil then reduce the heat and simmer away for as long as you have – anything from 30 minutes to a couple of hours.

Strain through a sieve and you're done!

Let the stock cool before storing in the fridge (for up to 5 days) or the freezer (for several months) in a plastic container.

If space is an issue, return the strained stock to the pan and boil hard to reduce the volume by three-quarters. It should now be brown and strong-tasting. Freeze in an ice-cube tray, then pop out and store in a plastic bag: ready-made stock cubes!

chicken stock

You can use the remains of a roast chicken or, even better, a raw chicken carcass. In either case, try to break it up a bit before putting it in the pot. If you don't have time to use your chicken carcass for stock you can freeze it. In fact it makes sense to wait until you have two or three stored up, provided you have a stock pot big enough to fit them all in. Chicken wings are fantastic for flavour, too, and are cheap. As with vegetable stock, use a selection of vegetables and herbs - carrots, onion and celery plus parsley, bay and thyme are the classic veg and herb trios.

Start by placing just the chicken in the pot and covering with cold water. Slowly bring to a boil and use a spoon or strainer to skim off the scum that rises.

Now add the vegetables and herbs, reduce the heat and let it simmer very gently for at least 1 hour and preferably 3.

Lift out the bigger bits of chicken carcass with a slotted spoon or tongs then strain the stock through a sieve.

If you'd like to remove the fat, let it rise to the surface and then skim it off with a spoon. A good chef's tip is to swirl the bottom of a ladle over the surface of the stock in ever-increasing circles to push the fat to the edges, then quickly use the ladle to scoop it up. Or chill the stock overnight and simply lift the solidified fat off the top. But you might not want to bother: chicken fat tastes great and is full of nutrients.

Reduce and store the stock as described opposite for vegetable stock.

TIP
Save any skimmed-off chicken fat for frying potatoes.

vinaigrettes

There are two main things to bear in mind when making your salad dressings: firstly, everyone has their favourite, so take this basic recipe and adjust the quantities until you find your perfect mix; secondly, the flavour of dressings is diluted when tossed with your salad leaves, so when tasting it neat, you're looking for a punchy flavour.

quick & easy   vegan

basic vinaigrette

Vinaigrette will keep in the fridge for a week or so. Taste it again before using as it will likely have lost some of its zing and may need a little more vinegar. This quantity of vinaigrette will probably do you two or three salads.

2 tbsp red wine vinegar
2 tsp Dijon mustard
½ garlic clove, crushed (optional)
pinch of sugar
pinch of salt
a few grindings of black pepper
6 tbsp extra virgin olive oil

Whisk everything except the oil together in a bowl until well combined.

Pour in the oil while continuing to whisk: it should emulsify into a thick, creamy consistency.

Alternatively, vigorously shake everything together in a jam jar.

Taste and add more sugar, salt, pepper or mustard if desired.

VARIATIONS

* Try different vinegars – white wine, cider, balsamic, sherry and walnut are all good – or a mixture. Or replace the vinegar with lemon juice, or a mixture of lemon and orange juice.

* Try different oils – a good rapeseed oil will add a nice nutty flavour and walnut oil also makes a fantastic vinaigrette.

* Try different mustards, e.g. wholegrain, or leave it out altogether. Or replace the mustard with a teaspoon of prepared horseradish – great for beetroot salads.

* Try honey instead of sugar, or leave it out.

* Replace the garlic with some very finely diced shallot, or use both.

* Whizz the vinaigrette in a blender or processor to incorporate soft herbs such as basil, tarragon, chives or chervil: it will go bright green and taste amazing.

* A few ground spices work well in some salads, e.g. fennel with orange and kohlrabi, cumin with beetroot and carrot, paprika with chickpeas and butterbeans.

* Make it creamy by substituting buttermilk, yoghurt, crème fraîche, soured cream or a mix of these for the oil. You may want to reduce the vinegar slightly.

* Indulge in a brown-butter dressing, which is delicious on green leaves and vegetables such as broccoli. Melt around 50g butter in a frying pan and continue cooking until the milk solids turn nut-brown. Whisk together with the vinegar and seasonings and use immediately, before the butter solidifies.

mayonnaise

You have several options for how to make mayonnaise - in a food processor, by hand or in a stand mixer (or using a hand-held electric whisk). Purists say it has a better texture and flavour when made by hand. If you're just making a small amount, and there are two of you, this is really not so hard. But for a big batch we recommend using a mixer or electric whisk as it's so quick and easy.

quick & easy

vegetarian

basic mayonnaise

Make sure all the ingredients are at room temperature as this helps them emulsify. Mayonnaise can be kept in the fridge in a jar for a few days.

MAKES ABOUT 250ML

1 egg (separated if making by hand)
good pinch of salt
1 tsp Dijon mustard, or more to taste
juice of ½ lemon
50ml light olive oil
200ml sunflower oil (or less for a thinner mayo)

To make in a food processor

Using a whole egg makes a less conventional, thinner mayonnaise, but if you're using a food processor it helps prevent the mayonnaise becoming too gloopy with the fast action of the machine. Crack the egg into the bowl, add the salt, mustard and 2 teaspoons of lemon juice and blend together. Then, with the motor running, slowly drizzle in the olive oil. Continue with the sunflower oil until it looks like mayonnaise and has reached the desired consistency. Taste and blend in more salt, lemon juice and mustard as desired.

To make by hand

Place the egg yolk only in a bowl, add the salt, mustard and 2 teaspoons of lemon juice and blend together using a balloon whisk. The lemon and mustard will both help the mayonnaise emulsify, so we recommend adding them now, at the beginning. While continuing to whisk, slowly drizzle in a little olive oil. Continue whisking and drizzling – a job most easily done by two people – and slowly increase the rate at which you pour in the oil. Continue with the sunflower oil until it has all been used. If the mixture gets very thick and difficult to whisk, mix in a little lukewarm water and continue. Taste and blend in more salt, lemon juice and mustard as desired.

TIP
If the mixture splits – that is to say, comes out of its creamy emulsion and looks horribly wrong – start again in a new bowl with a new egg yolk and slowly whisk in the split mayonnaise from your first attempt, then continue with more oil if needed.

VARIATIONS

* For a stronger, more peppery mayo, use more olive than sunflower oil, or equal quantities. Or for a different flavour altogether and lovely yellow colour, use a good rapeseed oil. One large egg yolk can take up to around 300ml of oil.

* Use vinegar instead of lemon juice – cider and white wine vinegars are best.

* Add crushed garlic to make aioli and/ or smashed salted anchovies for a delicious anchovy mayo. Both options are great with crudités.

* Add lots of chopped herbs at the end – basil, tarragon, chives, chervil and dill are particularly good. Or whizz a bunch of soft herbs, stems and all, with warm oil and then strain through a sieve to make a bright green, flavoured oil to use in your mayo. Herby mayos are especially good with a chicken salad.

* Thin it into a salad cream with soured cream or buttermilk.

* Experiment! Consider tomato purée, Tabasco, cayenne, saffron, chopped capers, prepared horseradish, lime juice and zest... but not all at once!

Index

Acknowledgements

The Riverford community is extensive. Over the years, the good will and generosity of countless customers, staff and friends have helped us evolve a cooking style and a bank of recipes to maintain our enthusiasm for season after season of beans and broccoli, courgettes and cardoons.

Special thanks for bringing this book to fruition to Kirsty Hale, the backbone of our recipe team for many years and tireless inventor of better ways with veg; to Anna Colquhoun, a founder Riverford Cook who gives generously of her time and shares her enthusiasm for the anthropology as well as the practicalities of food; and to Rob Andrew, longstanding Riverford chef with an inventive knowledge of veg built up in his years at Riverford (Field Kitchen, Travelling Field Kitchen, staff canteen) and before.

Imogen Fortes has been a firm, supportively critical and knowledgeable editor. Ariel Cortese, of Big Fish, has contributed the beautiful art work, and Alex and Emma Smith, of Smith & Gilmour, the design, cover and art direction.

Thank you to Ali Allen for most of the wonderful food photography, Emily Jonzen for the food styling and Martin Ellis for the rich bank of photos he has built up to represent life at Riverford through the seasons.

Finally, my sister, Rachel Watson, has been the guiding inspiration behind what we hope will become a series of books that will keep customers happily exploring and exploiting their veg boxes for many years to come.

Cataloguing in Publication Data is available from
the British Library

ISBN 978-0-9932155-1-3

Design and art direction: Smith & Gilmour
Project editor: Imogen Fortes
Recipe photography: Ali Allen
Landscape and farm photography: Martin Ellis
Still life photography: James Murphy
Font design and illustration: Ariel Cortese at Big Fish
Food styling: Emily Jonzen and Kirsty Hale
Prop styling: Emma Lahaye

Linen provided by The Linen Works

Printed and bound in Italy by L.E.G.O.

www.riverford.co.uk

autumn plenty
September to November

beans (runner)
broccoli (Calabrese)
cabbage
   (Savoy; tundra)
carrots
cauliflower
   (inc. Romanesco)
cavolo nero/
   black kale
chard
fennel
kale (curly;
   red Russian)
leeks

onions
parsnips
potatoes
   (pink fir apple;
   Orla; Cosmos; Desiree)
pumpkin
radicchio
salad leaves
spinach
squashes (butternut;
   crown prince; kabocha;
   spaghetti)
sweetcorn
watercress